The Impact of Economic Reforms on Rural Households in Ethiopia

A STUDY FROM 1989 TO 1995

POVERTY DYNAMICS IN AFRICA

POVERTY DYNAMICS IN AFRICA SERIES

This volume is one of a series of studies completed under the Poverty Dynamics in Africa Initiative, which is organized by the Africa Region of the World Bank. This initiative has received support from several bilateral donors: Italy, the Netherlands, Switzerland, the United Kingdom, and the United States. The motive for the series, launched in 2002, was to make use of the vastly improved household survey data in Africa and to enhance understanding of poverty trends on this continent during the 1990s. The goal is to provide a more secure empirical basis on which to assess past progress in poverty reduction in Africa, and to frame more effective policies for the future.

The countries selected for investigation are those in which the household survey data are robust and can sustain comparisons over time. Many of the studies focus on income (or consumption) poverty and seek to link poverty outcomes to wider economic change in the countries concerned, including economic policy reforms. Other studies use demographic and health surveys, which have provided invaluable information about the well-being of African people—especially the children. Further information can be obtained from the Poverty Reduction and Economic Management (PREM) unit in the Africa Region of the World Bank.

The Impact of Economic Reforms on Rural Households in Ethiopia

A STUDY FROM 1989 TO 1995

POVERTY DYNAMICS IN AFRICA

Stefan Dercon

THE WORLD BANK
Washington, D.C.

Cover design: Naylor Design, Inc., Washington, D.C.
Cover photo credit: Ray Witlin; Ethiopia

ISBN 0-8213-5034-X

Library of Congress Cataloging-in-Publication Data has been applied for.

Contents

Acknowledgments   *vii*

Abbreviations and Acronyms   *viii*

Abstract   *ix*

INTRODUCTION   1

PART 1: ECONOMIC REFORM IN RURAL ETHIOPIA:
  A DESCRIPTIVE ANALYSIS   7

  1. Reforms and Macroeconomic Performance 1989–95   9
  2. Economic Reforms and the Rural Economy 1989–95   12
  3. Study Villages 1989–95   24
  4. Economic Reform and the Village Economy   37

PART 2: EXPLAINING GROWTH AND POVERTY CHANGES   51
  5. Methodology for Decomposing Growth and Poverty Changes   53
     Decomposing Income   53
     Linking Poverty and Growth: Simulating the Impact of Variables   56
     Simulating and Decomposing the Impact of a Group of
     Variables   59
     Linking Poverty and Growth: An Overall Assessment   60
  6. Econometric Model and Results   64
  7. Explaining Real Income Changes of the Poor   82
  8. Decomposing Poverty Changes   90
  9. Conclusions   98

REFERENCES   102

TABLES
1. GDP per Capita and Other Macroeconomic Indicators, 1982–98   11
2. Evolution of Real Teff Prices   14
3. Coffee Tax, Marketing Costs, and Overvaluation: Percentage Effects on Farmgate Prices   17
4. Comparison of the ERHS and the HICES-WMS   25
5. Villages and Their Characteristics   25
6. Income Sources in 1994 as Percentages of Total Gross Income   28
7. Food Sales and Purchases   29
8. Percentage of Rainfall, Relative to Mean   31
9. Changes in Food Consumption per Month per Adult Equivalent between 1989 and 1994–95, in Birr and in 1994 Prices   32
10. Poverty between 1989 and 1994–95   33
11. Real Producer Prices: Percentage Increases Relative to 1989   38
12. Selected Changes in Land Allocation, 1989–94   40
13. Export Crop Expansion, 1983–95   41
14. Evolution in Fertilizer Use, 1989–94   42
15. Involvement in Off-Farm Activities: Percentage of Households Reporting to Be Involved   44
16. Real Incomes per Year per Adult, in Birr and in 1994 Prices   45
17. Asset Values and Changes, 1989–94   46
18. Econometric Model Real Income Function: Dependent Variable Was Change in Log Consumption between 1989 and 1994   70
19. Decomposition of Real Consumption Growth   72
20. Robustness Test: Using Real Income with and without Livestock Sales Income   77
21. Decomposition of Income Regression (Table 20) as a Percentage of Total Contribution   78
22. Household Characteristics by Poverty Transition Group   84
23. Explaining Consumption Changes by Poverty Transition Group   88
24. Microsimulations of the Total Impact of Different Factors on Poverty (Normalized Watts Poverty Index)   91
25. Decomposition of the Poverty Gap (Normalized Watts Poverty Index)   92
26. Poverty Decomposition by Village: Percentage Point Contribution to Total Decline in the Poverty Gap   94
27. Decomposition of Growth per Adult and Poverty Gap: Percentage Point Contribution to Total Growth   95

Acknowledgments

The research in this text uses data collected by the Department of Economics at Addis Ababa University and the Centre for the Study of African Economies at Oxford University, as well as by the International Food Policy Research Institute in Washington, D.C. The data collection was financed by the Swedish International Development Agency, the Economic and Social Research Council, United Kingdom, and the Fund for Scientific Research, Belgium.

This work would have been impossible without the dedicated efforts of numerous members and associates in the Department of Economics at Addis Ababa University, for which I am very grateful. I have benefited from discussions with and useful comments by John Hoddinott, Peter Lanjouw, Hans Elbers, Lionel Demery, François Bourguignon, Denis Cogneau, and seminar audiences at Leuven, Oxford, WIDER Helsinki, Amsterdam, and INRA/Paris. This study was conducted as part of the Poverty Dynamics in Africa study. All errors are my own.

Abbreviations and Acronyms

AISCO	Agricultural Input Supply Corporation
AMC	Agricultural Marketing Corporation
CPI	Consumer price index
ECMC	Ethiopian Coffee Marketing Corporation
EPLF	Eritrean People's Liberation Front
EPRDF	Ethiopian People's Revolutionary Democratic Front
ERHS	Ethiopian Rural Household Survey
FAO	Food and Agriculture Organization of the United Nations
FFW	Food for work
GDP	Gross domestic product
HICES	Household Income and Consumption Expenditure Survey
IMF	International Monetary Fund
NGO	Nongovernmental organization
OLF	Oromo Liberation Front
OLS	Ordinary least squares
TPLF	Tigrayan People's Liberation Front
WMS	Welfare Monitoring Survey

Abstract

n the late 1980s, the Ethiopian economy was very fragile. Famine, years of civil war, high rural taxation, and price and marketing controls had taken their toll, especially in rural areas. The demise of the Communist paymasters after the fall of the Berlin Wall meant that the situation was unsustainable. Food markets were liberalized from 1988. The civil war ended with the fall of the Communist government in 1991. Subsequently, further market liberalization and a large currency devaluation took place. Household panel data from six rural communities were used to study the impact of these reforms on growth and poverty in the period from 1989 to 1995.

Locally, growth outperformed the average growth rate in gross domestic product. Using an absolute measure of poverty, the author found that overall poverty decreased relatively strongly. Nevertheless, poverty remains high in most communities. A significant number of households saw their welfare decrease in this period as well; some even experienced a move into poverty. Can the changes in welfare and poverty be explained by reform-induced higher returns to physical and human capital? Or, are poverty decreases superficial; for example, are poverty gains simply related to better weather in some communities? To answer these questions, the author uses a profit function framework to explain growth using prices and endowments of land, labor, human capital, and location characteristics, while he controls for shocks. Next he develops a regression-based decomposition of the changes in the poverty gap. It is found that common and idiosyncratic shocks matter, but that the main factors driving consumption changes are relative price changes, resulting in changes in the returns to land, labor, human capital, and location. A detailed discussion of the factors that may have contributed to these changes supports the view that reforms have helped. Producer prices increased in most areas, while incentives for market-based activities contributed as well— the latter most likely aided by increased security. Locally, and against the national trend, the agroclimatic conditions were not much better in the five preceding years, while in some villages, the most recent rains in 1994 were rather bad. The poor have benefited more from the reforms, on average, than have the nonpoor households, suggesting that the reforms have been rather pro-poor. But the experience of the poor is mixed. One group in 1989, with relatively good land and labor, as well as access to roads and towns, strongly outperformed all other households, while also experiencing the best weather. Another group, with much poorer endowments, also faced poor rains and smaller producer price increases, resulting in virtually unchanged and persistent poverty.

Introduction

n the last few decades, Ethiopia has experienced turbulent times. In 1974, a revolution led by the military resulted in the removal of the emperor from power. Soon afterwards, a military government, subsequently known as the "Derg" (meaning the committee), came to power, with Col. Mengistu Hailemariam becoming, in due course, its undisputed leader. This government initiated important reforms, most strikingly a large land reform that removed feudal landlords from controlling large parcels of rural land. Land became state owned, but rural households were offered the right to till the land for their own benefit. Most large private companies became nationalized, while price controls and trading restrictions were imposed, most notably on agricultural produce. During this period, cold war politics led to a strict alignment with the Soviet Union and Eastern European communist states, which further influenced the nature and structure of the economy. Dissent was crushed during a period of large-scale repression in the late 1970s, known as the "Red Terror."

During the 1980s, Ethiopia was faced with a number of crises. A widespread famine occurred in 1984–85 in large parts of the country, but mainly in the north. Separatist and other anti-government movements intensified their civil war against government forces, mainly in Eritrea and in the northern province of Tigray. By the late 1980s, with the fall of the Berlin Wall and the subsequent changes in Russia and Eastern Europe, finances for the war and for the economy dried up, putting serious pressure on the macroeconomy and the regime itself. The intensification of the war in the north brought more and more success for the anti-government groups. In 1991, a coalition led by the Tigrayan People's Liberation Front (TPLF) took Addis Ababa, which defeated the Derg and its leader, who fled to Zimbabwe. Just before that, in Eritrea, the Eritrean People's Liberation Front (EPLF) had taken control and prepared for the independence of Eritrea. Despite some further internal conflict in Ethiopia—notably brief but intense fighting with the Oromo Liberation Front (OLF) in 1992—a period of relative peace ensued. This period lasted until the intense and costly border conflict with Eritrea in the late 1990s.

Even before the end of the civil war in 1991, the economic crisis and the disappearance of the erstwhile paymasters had instigated some economic reforms. Since 1988, Ethiopia has moved gradually from a communist-inspired, controlled economy to a more market-based economy. The first measures involved the abolition of high rural taxes and trade restrictions related to food crops, as well as some recognition of the role of the private sector in the economy. In 1992, further measures were taken, including a large devaluation and the first steps toward a more liberalized economy, through the gradual removal of trade restrictions and a reform of the investment code. These reforms became part of a structural adjustment program sponsored by the International Monetary Fund (IMF) and the World Bank in 1994.

Much has been written about the consequences of structural adjustment on growth and poverty (Cornia, Jolly, and Stewart 1987; Demery and Squire 1996; Sahn 1994, 1996). New evidence on the role of growth on poverty alleviation has revived the debate on how economic reform affects the poor (Dollar and Kraay 2000; Ravallion and Datt 2000; Srinivasan 2000). Most studies imply that the lack of data is a problem; systematic microeconomic evidence remains limited on both growth and poverty after market reforms take place.

A panel data set on 362 rural households in six communities, which was collected in 1989 and in 1994–95, is used for this text. This data set is small and is not a representative sample of rural Ethiopia; the villages in the data set were chosen because they had suffered in one way or another from the 1984–85 famine (Webb, von Braun, and Yohannes 1992). Consequently, the results listed here should not be viewed as evidence of overall poverty trends. The focus of this text is on the link between reforms, growth, and changes in poverty. The text provides evidence on the mechanisms by which, given the current conditions and policies, growth is translated into rural poverty alleviation.[1]

Methodologically, this study differs substantially from other studies in the literature (for reviews, see Lipton and Ravallion 1995; Azam 1994). Some studies limit themselves to outcome indicators at different points in time and use a macroeconomic narrative to argue that observed changes are the consequence of policy changes (for one such study, see Demery and Squire 1996). A criticism of such studies is that they cannot separate the effects of the reforms from other factors, such as external shocks or the lagging consequences of past recessions. Computable general equilibrium models can avoid these problems by allowing the impact of different counterfactual scenarios to be evaluated. Sahn (1996) presents a collection of such studies (earlier attempts are in Bourguignon, de Melo, and Morrisson 1991). Drawbacks of general equilibrium models are the immense data requirements and the strong structure that needs to be imposed on such models, which result in questions about the realism involved. Other studies are sectoral in nature and provide detailed evidence on the effects of reforms on particular activities; examples include the multimarket studies (Braverman and Hammer 1986). These sectoral studies provide important information but may be inconclusive about the overall impact on household incomes and consumption. More specifically, while their simulations give information on some of the income sources of households, the overall effects on incomes of different households, taking into account all activities and income sources, cannot be directly assessed.

By using comparable data sets over time, more detailed analysis is possible, not just of outcome indicators, but also of other factors. For example, Grootaert (1995) uses detailed socioeconomic characteristics to check whether, in different periods of the adjustment process in Côte d'Ivoire, the evidence is consistent with reforms driving the outcomes. Alternatively, econometric approaches can help control for other factors driving the outcome (other than the reforms), provided that the necessary information is available. In the context of Ethiopia, an important issue about rural outcomes is whether they are driven by different weather conditions in different years or by changing economic incentives. This issue can be clarified by controlling for common and idiosyncratic shocks in regressions using panel data. Nevertheless, when only repeated cross-section data sets are available, and sufficient detail is available in the survey data to model the changing determinants of outcomes, much analysis can still be done. For instance, microeconomic simulation approaches can then provide useful insights into the microeconomic link between income growth and poverty (the study by Bourguignon, Fournier, and Grugnand 2001 provides an example). This text uses a similar approach, but panel data have certain econometric advantages and provide direct information on the movements of individuals across the welfare distribution, rather than estimated movements.

Generalizing about the effects of macroeconomic and market-oriented reforms on poverty is difficult. Such measures as devaluation or liberalization have a priori ambiguous effects on welfare (Kanbur 1987). For example, a real exchange rate depreciation increases prices to the tradable goods sector relative to the nontradable sector, but the effect on welfare for particular groups will depend on whether their earnings relative to their consumption are geared more to goods from one sector than to another. If the poor produce or earn a wage from tradables and they mainly consume nontradables, then they will benefit. However, whether this indeed characterizes the poor cannot be stated in general (Lipton and Ravallion 1995). Furthermore, typical economic reforms, such as those in Ethiopia, involve many measures, including internal market reforms, which affect different households and regions differently. Finally, even if market prices move favorably for particular households, the net welfare effects of these price changes depend on the functioning of other markets. De Janvry, Sadoulet, and Fafchamps(1991) have analyzed and illustrated, using simulations, that the supply responsiveness to increased tradables prices is strongly dependent on whether any factor and goods markets are missing or imperfect. Clearly, to understand the effects of general macroeconomic measures on households, a careful and local analysis of both relative price movements and local market functioning is needed.

To facilitate data collection, the survey focused on a limited number of villages. We can exploit this feature to develop a village-level, economic narrative of the changing conditions in the local economy, such as in actual changes in the relative prices faced, similar to the *macroeconomic* narrative used to assess the information on households in many of the earlier studies. In the end, what is lost in terms of general assumptions, because of the relatively small sample, is gained in terms of understanding the way local conditions and context affect outcomes. Several sections of this text are devoted to describing these changing local conditions.

The panel provides highly comparable data on (food) consumption, assets, infrastructure, activity choice, household composition, and the like. Income data are available as well, although there are reasons to believe that these data are less reliable, especially in terms of comparability over time, than are the other data in the survey. Nevertheless, since the general trends in the income data are consistent with the other data sources, they help to establish the robustness of the findings. Input data are generally incomplete, so analysis of production functions and other structural models was not feasible. As a consequence, the analysis is confined to reduced-form analysis using an overall household profit function; that is, welfare changes are directly linked to fixed endowments and prices. Changes in the returns to assets can be approximately measured but with incomplete evidence on how reforms or other factors may have encouraged any changes in the allocation of inputs to different activities.

The main conclusions of this study can be summarized as follows: Locally, growth outperformed the average growth rate in gross domestic product (GDP). Using an absolute measure of poverty, overall poverty decreased relatively strongly. Nevertheless, poverty remains high in most communities. A significant number of households saw their welfare decrease and some experienced a move into poverty during this period. From the regressions it is clear that common and idiosyncratic shocks matter, but that the main factors driving shifts in consumption are relative price changes, which result in changes in the returns to land, labor, human capital, and location. A detailed discussion of the factors that may have contributed to these changes supports the view that reforms have helped. Producer prices increased in most areas, while incentives for market-based activities contributed as well—the latter most likely aided by increased security. Against the national trend, the local agroclimatic conditions were not much better between 1989 and 1995 than in the five preceding years, while in some villages, the most recent rains in 1994 failed.

Poor households have benefited more from the reforms on average than have nonpoor households, which suggests that the reforms have been pro-poor. However, the experience of the poor was mixed. One group of people identified as poor in 1989 and who had relatively good land and labor, access to roads and towns, and the best weather strongly outperformed all other households during the study period, 1989–95. Another group identified as poor in 1989, and with much poorer endowments, faced poor rains and smaller producer price increases, which resulted in virtually unchanged and persistent poverty during the study period.

The text is divided into two parts. Part 1 (chapters 1 to 4) is largely descriptive; part 2 (chapters 5 to 9) presents econometric analysis of the factors determining growth and poverty. In chapter 1 the evolution of the macroeconomy during 1989–95 is covered. Chapter 2 discusses the reforms, including a detailed analysis of the likely effects on the rural economy. Chapter 3 turns to the sample villages, presents the socioeconomic context of these communities, and lists details on shocks and events. Chapter 4 discusses the changes in returns and incentives experienced by these communities during this period, using an analysis of local relative price changes. Chapter 5 explains the framework for the econometric analysis, which focuses on specifying a model of income growth and linking it to a decomposition of poverty declines into changes in endowments, prices, and shocks. Chapter 6 presents the econometric results, including a decomposition of the factors contributing to growth. Chapters 7 and 8 give the results in terms of a decomposition of the poverty changes during this period of growth. Chapter 9 is the conclusion.

NOTE

1. A comparison with a nationally representative survey is given in chapter 3.

PART 1

Economic Reform in Rural Ethiopia

A Descriptive Analysis

Reforms and Macroeconomic Performance 1989–95

The 1980s was a period of crisis in Ethiopia. Since the late 1970s, the urban economy had been organized into a state-controlled, planned economy. The rural economy was largely ignored and heavily taxed. The Mengistu government imposed direct taxes and levies of various kinds on peasants, and forced them to work on community development projects or other activities determined by the state. During this period, the government also insisted that a regular and specified quota of grain be delivered to a parastatal corporation, the Agricultural Marketing Corporation (AMC). Bans and restrictions on private grain trade and trade in export crops were the equivalent of implicit taxation. In the mid-1980s, famine and war precipitated a major humanitarian disaster and a suffering economy. The fall of the Berlin Wall and subsequent political and economic events facing the regime's Communist sponsors led to a serious economic crisis in Ethiopia. In 1988, economic reforms began, initiated by the beleaguered government.

Between 1989 and 1994, there was considerable economic and political change in Ethiopia. First, a new political regime emerged at the end of the civil war in 1991 and replaced the Mengistu government. A coalition of anti-Derg forces, the Ethiopian People's Revolutionary Democratic Front (EPRDF), with the TPLF as a main partner, formed the new government. Security was largely restored in most parts of the country, at least until the late 1990s. Second, market reform had just started in food markets in 1989. In this same period—after the government's declaration of the mixed economy in 1988—encouragement of market-based activities began, with some incentives for private sector activities. In 1992, the birr was devalued by 142 percent and foreign exchange rationing gradually lessened. No inflationary effects followed from the devaluation, in part because of good harvests. In 1992 Ethiopia had close to zero inflation, and low inflation in subsequent years has meant a strong depreciation of the real exchange rate. In 1992, fertilizer market reform was started with the gradual removal of subsidies.

Data from the National Accounts show the changing fortunes of the Ethiopian economy. Table 1 gives data on total real GDP per capita in addition to private consumption per capita, government revenue and consumption, and gross capital formation per capita. The series are, in real terms, deflated by the GDP deflator.[1] They are listed as an index, with 1989 equal to 100. The GDP data show first the dramatic collapse of the economy during the famine of 1985, then a recovery followed by a further collapse during the transition period at the end of the civil war in 1991. By 1995 the economy, in per capita terms, was more or less back to the same level it was at the end of the 1980s. Subsequent growth has meant that Ethiopia has finally passed its 1982 level of per capita GDP.

This evolution of GDP per capita hides some important composition changes in this period. The collapse in Ethiopian GDP per capita in the mid-1980s was driven by the collapse in agricultural GDP. But agricultural GDP per capita did not fall significantly during the transition period of 1991–93. Private consumption bore its share of the decline in GDP in the mid-1980s. The picture is also different during the transition that occurred near the end of the civil war in 1991. The decline in overall GDP is attributed to a collapse in government expenditure, driven by a lapsed revenue collection, and a large fall in gross investment. Deflated private consumption per capita continued to rise; by 1995, it was just under 14 percent higher than in 1989. Gross investment also recovered quickly, but the share of government consumption in GDP was much slower.

Overall, this pattern provides some interesting facts for our analysis. First, there is evidence of limited growth in GDP per capita but increased private consumption at the expense of the government during our study period. Agricultural GDP per capita also grew during this period, albeit at a more modest

Table 1. GDP per Capita and Other Macroeconomic Indicators, 1982–98

Time period	Real GDP per capita[a]	Real consump- tion per capita[b]	Real government revenue per capita[c]	Real government consumption per capita[c]	Real gross capital formation per capita[c]	Real agricultural GDP per capita[d]
1982–84	103	110	78	87	101	122
1985–87	93	100	72	74	92	98
1988–90	101	101	90	98	111	102
1991–93	92	104	44	57	70	101
1994–96	99	114	66	56	117	103
1997–98	106	118	82	68	128	105

Note: 1989 = 100.

a. GDP per capita in constant 1980–81 prices. (Population figures are unclear for this period in Ethiopia. The war during the 1980s and suspicions about ethnic manipulations imply problems with the 1984 census estimates. The secession of Eritrea in 1993 complicates intertemporal estimates of GDP and population. A population census took place in 1994 that resulted in a downward revision of the population figures. Different sources [such as the U.S. Bureau of the Census, the IMF, and the World Bank] give different time series. A revision of the procedures governing the calculation of GDP complicates intertemporal comparisons further. As a result, other sources have different long-term series on GDP per capita. For example, World Bank series suggest a deeper collapse in 1985–87 but also a stronger recovery in 1997–98 to levels above the 1982–84 level.)

b. Private consumption in national accounts per capita, deflated by the GDP deflator. If deflated by the consumer price index, the outcome is very similar, except for a stronger recovery in 1997–98.

c. Government revenue, government consumption, and gross capital formation per capita, deflated by the GDP deflator.

d. Calculated from real growth data from the World Bank.

Source: International Financial Statistics, IMF (2000).

rate, and without the apparent collapse during the transition period. It appears that the reduced taxation may well have had positive effects in rural areas as well. However, it would be wrong to attribute the decline in direct taxation to the economic reforms. Azam and others (1994) have argued that the collapse of revenue collection because of the war and the overthrow of the government was the main reason for the collapse in tax revenue. Nevertheless, the fact that the old scale of rural taxation was not reinstated after the end of the civil war is a reflection of the move toward a less controlled economy using reforms.

NOTE

1. This is obviously problematic, but because there was a lack of specific deflators for these series, this procedure was nevertheless used. Broadly speaking, the GDP deflator and the Consumer Price Index followed similar patterns, but neither is directly relevant for government and investment expenditures.

CHAPTER 2

Economic Reforms and the Rural Economy 1989–95

The economic reform program that began in 1989 is likely to have had a strong impact on the Ethiopian rural economy. Those reforms need to be covered in some detail. First, continuous land reform was abolished in 1989. Before 1989, land could legally be taken away from households at any time, for example, to accommodate newly formed or growing households. When the new EPRDF government came to power in 1991, they reaffirmed a commitment to land tenure security. However, since then land has been confirmed as state property. Constitutionally, citizens have the right to lease land. Households supposedly get land on a long-term basis, but some recent episodes of new land redistribution have caused some anxiety about continuing land security. If anything, the end to continuous land redistribution has resulted in difficulties for young and newly formed households to acquire land (Ayalew, Dercon, and Krishnan 1999). In short, in the period under consideration, 1989–1995, the changes in land tenure security have had a mixed impact on output and welfare.

Food market reform began in 1990. Its consequences are likely to have been much more important for rural households than any changes in land tenure. Two measures of food market reform stand out: the removal of the quota system for farmers and the removal of trade taxes and restrictions (Azam 1993, 1996; Dercon 1994). First, the requirement that farmers deliver a predetermined quantity of specific grain, referred to as a quota, to the Agricultural Marketing Corporation (AMC) was cancelled. Between 1980 and 1990, farmers were required to deliver between 50 and 100 percent of their output to the AMC; they could sell the rest on the open market. While some farmers appear to have been exempt from this quota, in 1988 most farmers in the sample delivered grain (depending on local circumstances, teff, barley, sorghum, or maize) to the AMC.[1] The quota essentially imposed a tax on the farmer, since prices paid by the AMC were systematically lower than market prices. The main benefit of the quota's removal is a real income gain by farmers. Since the quota was a lump-sum tax, standard economic theory would predict no direct effect on output from this tax. However, since the quota levels to individual farmers were not fixed over time but could be reassigned, incentives to invest in agriculture were likely to be affected by this tax. Furthermore, and to the extent that there is a gap between local food sales and purchase prices, the quota may have reduced efficiency in agriculture, since the relative prices may induce farmers to grow crops they would not otherwise have chosen to grow.[2]

The effect of the quota system on prices is harder to predict. As a lump-sum tax, the quota system would have had only income effects, reducing the on-farm consumption of grain and therefore increasing total net sales (Azam 1994). Furthermore, the quota system is likely to have led to a net increase in the open market sales by farmers.[3] However, the quota system was meant to supply the urban areas, especially Addis Ababa, through Kebele shops.[4] Urban households could obtain a ration at the subsidized prices. The ration resulted in a pure income effect. Consequently, the removal of the ration would have reduced total grain consumption in urban areas; however, as long as non-grain consumption was normal, open market purchases increased. The overall result of liberalization then was higher supply and demand in the open market. The effect on prices is therefore ambiguous.

A second relevant measure of the reforms was the relaxation and later the abolition of restrictions on private grain trade. Unlike other African countries—and despite the anti–private sector attitude of the economic policy in the 1980s—private interregional trade was not banned, with the exception of a few surplus regions (such as Gojjam). Traders were, however, heavily taxed when trying to move grain around the country; they were forced to sell 50 percent or more of the quantity traded to the AMC at fixed prices below market value. The consequence of the traders' quota was to increase the marketing margins between different regions on the open market.[5] Liberalization would then have resulted in upward pressure on prices in surplus areas and downward pressure in deficit areas.

To what extent are these measures reflected in the evolution of food prices in this period? Data on the main staple grown for cash, teff, will be used to discuss this evolution. The best data sources since the mid-1980s are wholesale prices collected by the AMC; these data came from urban areas in the most important producer regions as well as in a few of the most important cities across the country.[6] For Addis Ababa, data series are available since 1980, while for other towns data are typically available only since 1987.

Table 2 reports on the evolution of real teff prices. Prices are deflated by the consumer price index (CPI) and given in 1990 prices.[7] The table shows that prices at the beginning of the 1990s were lower than prices in the 1980s, although it is important to note that harvests had been generally better in the 1990s. In the period 1990–92, the first few years after liberalization, prices had not yet come down, possibly because of the war. In the main deficit area, Addis Ababa, real prices did not increase after liberalization. The relative prices between Addis Ababa and other Ethiopian

Table 2. Evolution of Real Teff Prices

Time period	Price per kg.[a] Addis Ababa	Local price as a percentage of the Addis Ababa price								
		Deficit regions			Surplus regions					
		Dire Dawa	Dessie	Harar	Ambo	Debre Markos	Assela	Hosaenna	Nekempte	Shashemene
1981–83	1.53									
1984–86	1.92									
1987–89	1.48	119	91	130	73	52	72	61	67	74
1990–92	1.45	119	93	118	82	75	86	72	77	87
1993–95	1.31	119	103	120	92	88	93	82	86	95

Note: "Deficit" applies to towns in regions that are typically net importing; "surplus" applies to towns in regions that are typically net exporting.

a. Wholesale price per kilogram, in constant 1990 prices, using the consumer price index as a deflator. Source of the CPI is International Financial Statistics, IMF (2000).

Source: Calculated from Ethiopia Grain Trading Enterprise.

towns present more convincing evidence of the consequences of liberalization. In other large towns in deficit areas, the main trend (if any) appears to be a closing of the gap with Addis Ababa, in line with better market arbitrage possibilities following the abolition of taxes and trade restrictions. Relative to Addis Ababa, we find a systematic increase in prices, between 26 and 69 percent in real terms, in the typically surplus areas. The largest increase was found in Debre Markos, in Gojjam, one of the regions where interregional trade was totally banned, and the AMC had been given a monopoly. In general, this suggests a positive effect of liberalization on prices paid to farmers, probably without affecting net consumers much in deficit areas. Note that it may well have been the case that net consumers in surplus areas suffered from the liberalization.

Dercon (1995) analyzed further the evolution of grain prices in the period before and after liberalization. Using standard time series analysis of price dynamics in food markets, price series behavior before liberalization suggested that markets were slow to interconnect, which is consistent with a serious discouragement of private trade. After liberalization, most of the markets analyzed apparently experienced fast arbitrage between them. Transaction cost margins did not only decline between markets but arbitrage became faster as well, suggesting further increases in efficiency from the liberalization of food markets. Crucial for our analysis is that this text disentangles the effects from liberalization (which occurred in 1990) and those from the end of the war (in May 1991). The results showed that the larger impact on marketing margins came from the liberalization, and only on some routes did the end of the war have a significant impact.

A further result of market liberalization and improved arbitrage between regions appears to have offset the price fluctuations in certain markets. In particular, local seasonal effects are likely to have been reduced by stronger interregional interconnectedness. Although the available time series are relatively short, the reduction in seasonal fluctuations can be illustrated. Data are available for wholesale teff prices from 22 urban markets since 1987. In all markets, the ratio of the highest yearly price (in real terms) relative to the lowest price has decreased since 1991, compared to the period before 1990. The decline averages between 41 and 24 percent; the range declined from 32 and 103 percent to between 18 and 36 percent. In short, seasonal fluctuations appear to have been reduced considerably.

Another crucial measure for the rural economy was the devaluation of the birr in 1992. The official exchange rate of the Ethiopian birr had remained fixed since the 1970s at 2.07 birr to the U.S. dollar. Unlike most African countries, overvaluation in Ethiopia remained a relatively limited problem, even though the black market premium gradually grew to about 100 percent by the end of the 1980s. Inflation had remained relatively under control in this period—only during the famine year, 1985, was inflation above 10 percent.[8] However, during the political transition period, 1991–92, prices shot up by about 40 percent, and the black market exchange rate stood at above 6 birr. The devaluation of the birr in September 1992 resulted in an exchange rate of 5 birr to the dollar. In the subsequent twelve months, inflation did not pick up—in fact it was close to zero, while the black market rate moved to (only) about 7 birr. The real exchange rate depreciated consequently by a percentage very close to the nominal devaluation. In subsequent years, a gradual depreciation through the introduction of a managed auction system resulted in a relatively stable real exchange rate.[9] Between 1993 and 1998, it stood at about 36 percent of its 1989 level, while the black market premium has all but disappeared.[10]

The direct benefits of this real exchange rate depreciation for the rural economy would be in better prices for export crops, such as coffee, the most important export crop in Ethiopia. Increasing prices for imported goods—such as fertilizer, fuel, and certain consumer goods—may put extra costs on the rural economy. However, the effects are complicated by the presence of interventions in the marketing and pricing of commodities such as coffee, fertilizer, and fuel, as well as widespread black markets and smuggling of all commodities before the devaluation.

Coffee is only grown in a number of specific regions in the Ethiopian Highlands;[11] more than 90 percent of the production comes from smallholders. Coffee is not only exported, but large quantities are consumed domestically.[12] In fact, some farmers grow coffee only for home consumption. From the mid-1970s until recently, the government had tried to take full control of coffee pricing and marketing, especially regarding the export trade. Although private traders were permitted to operate, price controls existed at all levels of the marketing chain. The Ethiopian Coffee Marketing Corporation (ECMC) soon handled the trade of about 80 percent of the officially recorded trade in coffee. The coffee auctions in Addis Ababa and Dire Dawa, which operated as the main trading places for the large coffee traders before the 1974 revolution, were still operating, but prices at the auctions were in fact fixed by the Ministry of Coffee and Tea Development. After the fall of the Mengistu government in 1991, steps were taken to liberalize the coffee marketing, allowing traders to enter domestic markets more freely, although licenses remained expensive. The auction was allowed to function more freely. Export trade remained nevertheless controlled.

Substantial implicit and explicit taxes have been levied on coffee since the 1980s. Explicit taxes included a surtax, a transaction tax, and an export duty. Taxes were variable, increasing at higher world prices using a fixed formula. Implicit taxation included the cost of overvaluation and excessive marketing margins. Dercon and Ayalew (1995) studied these different taxes on farmers; table 3 summarizes their findings. During the 1980s, total taxes on farmers through the exchange rate, explicit tax, and excessive margins cut farmgate prices by a half to two-thirds. The largest tax was the export tax. By the end of the 1980s, export taxes became lower because of very low world prices, but overvaluation taxed the farmers quite heavily.

Table 3. Coffee Tax, Marketing Costs, and Overvaluation: Percentage Effects on Farmgate Prices

Item	Time period			
	1981–85	1986–89	1990–91	1992–93
Overvaluation (1)	0.22	0.07	0.48	−1.01
Explicit coffee tax (2)	0.38	0.34	0.04	0.04
Excessive marketing margin (3)	0.05	0.07	−0.19	0.62
Total tax rate on farmers: (1) + (2) + (3)	0.66	0.48	0.32	−0.35

Note: Calculations are based on an index of the price farmers would have received if there had been no taxes, no excessive marketing margins, and no overvaluation (that is, on a counterfactual coffee price). The basis for this counterfactual coffee price is the border price for coffee, but reflecting the international terms of trade for coffee; that is, in dollars using the nominal exchange rate divided by the manufacturing unit value index, and reflecting the marketing margin as it was in 1984–85, assumed to be reasonable. Denoting t as the explicit coffee tax, r as the effect of overvaluation, and m as the excessive marketing margin, then the relationship between the actual farmgate coffee price, AP, and the counterfactual price, CP, can be expressed as: $AP = (1-(t + r + m)) \times CP$. The calculations assume no overvaluation in 1970–71.

Source: Calculated from Dercon and Ayalew 1995, p.1803.

The high taxes, overvaluation, and excessive marketing margins encouraged the development of a parallel market for coffee, in which substantial quantities of coffee were smuggled. Dercon and Ayalew (1995) estimated that premiums from smuggling could have been as high as 300 percent during the 1980s. Smuggling was not without risk during this period. When arrests were made, harsh punishments were handed out. Furthermore, coffee collection for the marketing board was handled through the local service cooperative, essentially a local government-controlled institution, which also supplied key inputs, such as pesticides. In many areas the local service cooperative would have monitored farmers and limited their ability to smuggle. Dercon and Ayalew (1995) estimated, nonetheless, that about 10 to 15 percent of marketed production was smuggled.

The impact on farmers of the devaluation of 1992 has to be put against this background of smuggling. Table 3 shows that, relative to the 1970–71 real exchange rate, undervaluation provided a subsidy to coffee producers. However, a large part of the devaluation was absorbed by the marketing agents. In short, the farmgate price recovery may not be as substantial as the devaluation suggested. Furthermore, to the extent that smuggling was widespread, smuggling prices, rather than official prices, determined the incomes of many farmers. The relative stability of the black market exchange rate meant that the devaluation did not affect coffee prices for those farmers. Nevertheless, relative to the black market, the official farmgate prices were bound to improve, so some response in official supplies and export volumes was expected. This change in official supplies is likely to have come from switching volumes of coffee between channels, not from a production response, since new coffee trees take up to five years to mature and short-run productivity gains are unlikely.[13] The evidence suggests that a switch between channels indeed has happened. Export volumes in 1993–96 stood at about 83,000 metric tons on average, which is about 6,000 tons higher than levels during the period 1985–89; 6,000 tons is a relatively small amount, but it is in line with predictions on switching volumes back from the black market.[14] Since 1997, picked coffee export volumes have risen to higher levels than the levels of the early 1980s. Finally, in 1994 earnings from coffee increased because of the booming international coffee prices. Unit export values rose from 1994 to levels 65 percent higher than the historically low average prices of the period

1990–93. Although part of this increase was probably taken by the marketing agents, farmers are also likely to have benefited.

Other export crops were similarly affected; chat, in particular, deserves some mention.[15] During the 1980s, growing demand in surrounding countries resulted in a doubling of the chat border price at the official exchange rate. While still a small export crop relative to coffee, it has become popular throughout Ethiopia as a source of cash, and it is somewhat easier to grow than coffee. Chat has never been officially promoted, because of its addictive properties and the fact that it is illegal in most Western countries. The government's relative failure to regulate or promote this crop has meant that taxation has been limited, whereas smuggling has been relatively easy. For a crop such as chat, the devaluation has been relatively irrelevant.

As discussed previously, consumer prices did not increase after the devaluation. One important reason was that imports of many consumer goods had increasingly come into Ethiopia through the parallel (black) market, and this activity did not change markedly in the first few years after the devaluation. Other commodities, such as fuel, remained subsidized and increases were limited to levels below inflation over the study period. Using data from the Central Statistical Authority, rural fuel prices (kerosene for cooking) increased by only about 25 to 33 percent between 1989 and 1994, well below inflation. Transport in the CPI also increased by only about 40 percent in this period, well below the increase in the overall index (about 70 percent).

Fertilizer is another important imported commodity for rural Ethiopia. It was estimated that by 1995, about 31 percent of the farmers used chemical fertilizer; this represents about 37 percent of the cultivated land area (Mulat, Said, and Jayne 1998). Again, the market structure and subsidies limited the impact of the devaluation at first. The import and rural distribution of fertilizer remained a government monopoly until 1992, through the Agricultural Input Supply Corporation (AISCO). Since 1992, only a very limited number of private firms have entered the market. Some are close to parastatals of regional authorities, with local monopoly powers (Mulat, Said, and Jayne 1998). Fertilizer subsidies remained in place until 1997 and were only gradually phased out. Prices remained fixed by the government until then; in fact, the government continued to fix wholesale prices after the removal of subsidies, leaving only retail prices to be determined by the market operators. Prices still increased considerably, by about 80 to 100 percent for different types of fertilizers during the period 1988 to 1993, at a level just over the increase in consumer prices but well below the change in border prices at official exchange rates.[16] Since 1992, foreign aid and lower foreign exchange scarcity resulted in strong increases in availability, which further limited any effect of the higher prices.[17]

Although the private sector was officially encouraged to develop after the declaration of the "mixed economy" in 1988, liberalization measures remained relatively limited until the structural adjustment program began in 1992. Gradually most price controls were lifted, even though for most consumer goods, rationing and flourishing parallel markets made these measures less relevant for consumers, especially in rural areas. Import tariffs were also reduced considerably after 1994. Financial sector liberalization began in 1994, but its impact on the rural economy is still insignificant. Rural formal credit provision, beyond input credit, remains very small.

During the Derg, the development of other rural factor markets was discouraged. Agricultural wage labor, except in the formal economy, was, in principle, forbidden. Even though enforcement was likely to be limited, data from several communities suggest that this ban on wage labor was a serious hindrance for household income generation (Dercon and Krishnan 1998). Since the late 1980s and reaffirmed after the Mengistu government was defeated in 1991, wage labor was again allowed. To bring a collective element to agriculture, many area households had been expected to supply labor to agricultural or development activities. This practice was discontinued in the first few years after the fall of the Derg, but it seems to have reappeared.

A final benefit of the fall of the Mengistu government for rural areas is the collapse of tax collection in many areas and the subsequent lower tax burden on the rural economy. Taxes levied included an annual agricultural tax, membership fees for the peasant association, and various "voluntary" contributions. During the final years of the civil war, the government had introduced a large number of extra taxes to pay for the war effort (Webb, von Braun, and Yohannes 1992). In the last stages of the civil war, with revenue collection collapsing and general uncertainty, many of these taxes disappeared; only much later has rural taxation started again.[18] By the end of our study period in 1995, rural taxes were still very low.

NOTES

1. Local authorities could exempt certain households, such as landless households or those facing crop failure. In 1988, no quota was levied on Domaa, the resettlement village in the sample, but more than 80 percent of households report supplying the AMC in Dinki, Debre Berhan, and Adele Keke. Dessalegn (1991) reported that during the 1984–85 famine, some households were forced to buy grain from the market at an inflated price to supply the AMC, despite suffering serious crop failure.

2. If purchase and sales prices are the same, farmers could simply grow other crops, sell them, and buy the required quota.

3. To make this clear, suppose that the household produces total food H and consumes food C and manufactured goods M. Let the price of manufactured goods be the numéraire and p is the food price. With a ration q and quota price p_q, it follows that the budget constraint can be written as

$$(A.1) \qquad M + p \cdot C \le p \cdot H - \left(p - p_q\right) \cdot Q.$$

The lump-sum tax $(T\,(p,\,p_q,\,Q) = (p - p_q) \cdot Q)$ is an increasing function in Q and a decreasing function in p_q. Provided C and M are normal, increasing T meant reducing C and M. Since sales S equal $H - C$, it follows that since T has no effect on H, reducing the level of C—for example, by increasing Q—would have reduced S. Liberalization is then likely to have reduced the total marketed supply. Open market prices were, however, affected by the supply, net of the quota. For grain, it is likely that the quota system would have repressed open market supplies. Let sales to the open market F be defined as S, total sales, minus Q, the quota. The effect of increasing Q on F is positive if

$$(A.2) \qquad \frac{\partial F}{\partial Q} = \frac{\partial S}{\partial Q} - 1 > 0$$

which implies that

$$(A.3) \qquad \frac{\partial S}{\partial Q} = \frac{\partial C}{\partial Y} \cdot \left(p - p_q\right) > 1$$

or

(A.4) $$\varepsilon_\gamma \cdot b_g > \frac{p}{p - p_q}$$

in which ε_γ is the income elasticity of grain and b_g is the budget share of grain in total expenditure. Note that b_g is, by definition, smaller than one, and that the right side is strictly larger than one. It follows that the income elasticity of grain must be sufficiently larger than one for an increase in the quota to result in an increase in the supply to the open market. Since this is unlikely to be the case for the income elasticity of staples, the quota system is likely to have reduced open market supplies. Consequently, the abolition of the quota is likely to have led to an increase in the supplies to the open market.

4. The Kebele is the local administration of different neighborhoods in the cities.

5. To see this, let q be the quantity that traders need to supply when crossing regional borders between region i and j; let t_{ij} be the transport and marketing cost between i and j; let p_i (p_j) be the grain price in region i (region j) and trade is assumed to be profitable between i and j. Furthermore, let p_{qt} be the price paid by the AMC (lower than p_i) and t_{iq} be the transport cost up to the quota collection point ($t_{iq} < t_{ij}$). Then from the arbitrage conditions, it follows that trade will take place until $p_j - p_i = t_{ij} + q \cdot ((p_j - p_{qt}) - (t_{ij} - t_{iq}))$. In words, for $q > 0$ and if trading between i and j is more profitable than selling to the marketing parastatal, then price margins between net selling and net buying regions were higher because of the quota system.

6. The data were obtained from the Ethiopian Grain Trading Enterprise, which is effectively the renamed and reformed Agricultural Marketing Corporation.

7. A nonfood price index may have been more appropriate, but consistent disaggregated data series were available only until 1993. Up to this period, very little difference can be observed in the overall pattern by using a nonfood consumer price index.

8. Note that this is unlikely to have been caused by price controls, since prices were recorded in the open market, rather than in controlled state ration shops.

9. Calculated in its simplest way, this is the nominal exchange rate deflated by consumer prices.

10. The black market was revived by the outbreak of the hostilities between Ethiopia and Eritrea in 1998.

11. Mainly in the provinces of Sidamo, Keffa, Wellega, Illubabor, and Hararghe.

12. According to Food and Agriculture Organization (FAO) estimates, about 50 percent.

13. Aging trees, plant diseases, and poor extension make such short-run responses difficult. Dercon and Ayalew (1995) found evidence of a long-run supply elasticity of 0.10 percent to changing prices of coffee (relative to competing crops) but a virtual zero short-run elasticity. An aggregate supply response (that is, not relative to other crops) could not be detected.

14. Dercon and Ayalew (1995) estimated from their econometric model that about 5,000 to 15,000 tons would return to official channels if taxation, overvaluation, and excessive margins were removed.

15. Chat or q´at is a valuable amphetamine-type stimulant, increasingly popular in Ethiopia and in neighboring countries.

16. In net terms, farmers may have been paying much more for fertilizer by 1994 than this percentage increase. Most fertilizer sales are established on the basis of input credit. Many farmers and service cooperatives made use of the gradual collapse of the monopolist in agricultural credit supply, the Agricultural and Industrial Development Bank, in the last few years before the fall of the Mengistu government; loan recovery fell to 37 percent in 1991 and 15 percent in 1992. Furthermore, interest rates on input credit more than doubled in this period.

17. By 1995, the problem became the lack of demand at current prices, and most operators could sell only three-quarters, or even less, of their imported quantities (Mulat, Said, and Jayne 1998).

18. Given the poor state of public services in rural areas by the end of the 1980s, the collapse in expenditure is unlikely to have outweighed the benefits obtained from the collapse of revenue collection.

Study Villages 1989–95

The study uses data on six rural communities. Villages in the 1989 sample were selected because they had experienced the crisis and recovery from drought and famine in the mid-1980s (Webb, von Braun, and Yohannes 1992).[1] Within each village, the inhabitants were randomly sampled. In 1994, the specific households sampled in 1985 were reinterviewed as part of a larger sample survey, the Ethiopian Rural Household Survey (ERHS).[2] In this way, a panel of households was constructed, which forms the basis of this text. The attrition rate between 1989 and 1994 was surprisingly low; about 95 percent of households were successfully reinterviewed. Since 1994, several more rounds of interviews were completed. In this text, the focus is on data up to 1995, that is, the data collected in the three survey rounds from 1994–95. More details on the survey can be found in Dercon and Krishnan (1998).

The ERHS is a small sample and can hardly be called representative for Ethiopia as a whole. Its value is that it is a panel data set; in other words, it can be used to assess the determinants of changes over time. Nevertheless, it is useful to know how this sample compares with rural Ethiopia as a whole. In 1995–96, the Central Statistical Authority conducted a survey on a representative sample of 11,687 households, as part of the welfare monitoring efforts by the Government of Ethiopia. The survey collected information on consumption levels and household characteristics, by combining a Welfare Monitoring Survey (WMS) and the Household Income and Consumption Expenditure Survey (HICES). Table 4 compares the ERHS with the 1995–96 HICES-WMS (using only

Table 4. Comparison of the ERHS and the HICES-WMS

Item	Six villages in ERHS	HICES-WMS (rural), 1995–96
Observations (number of households)	352	7,408
Average household size (number)	6.1	5.1
Female-headed household (percent)	18	20
Stunting (below six years, percent)	52	68
Net primary enrollment rate, boys (percent)	14	16
Net primary enrollment rate, girls (percent)	9	9
Illiteracy rate of household head (percent)	69	75
Distance to primary school (kilometers)	3.2	4.3
Distance to health center (kilometers)	7.6	10

Note: ERHS = Ethiopian Rural Household Survey, HICES = Household Income and Consumption Expenditure Survey, and WMS = Welfare Monitoring Survey.

Table 5. Villages and Their Characteristics

Item	Village					
	Dinki	Debre Berhan	Adele Keke	Korodegaga	Gara Godo	Domaa
Region	Amhara	Amhara	Oromo	Oromo	Southern	Southern
Main crops	Sorghum, teff, maize	Barley, beans, wheat	Sorghum, maize, chat	Teff, maize, beans, barley	Maize, beans, coffee, enset	Maize, teff, enset
Altitude (m)	2,000	2,700	1,320	2,000	1,730	1,070
Mean rainfall (mm)[a]	1,664	919	753	874	944	1,117
Distance to nearest town (km)[b]	10	10	13	25	13	3.5
Type of road	Feeder	Highway	Tarmac	Dirt	Dirt	Feeder

a. Measured at the nearest rainfall station. No village-level measures are available. Despite a distance of only about 15 kilometers from the rainfall station, rainfall in Dinki is much lower than reported here because of specific conditions near the escarpment.

b. Distances are measured from the center of the village. This means that some households may live much farther than recorded. Distances are relative to a town with basic facilities, such as electricity, telephones, and transportation.

Source: ERHS Community Questionnaires.

the rural areas). In terms of outcomes, a reasonable fit exists between the two surveys.

The villages surveyed are located in the central and southern part of Ethiopia. In 1989, the civil war made it impossible to survey any northern villages. Nevertheless, the villages surveyed have many characteristics that are common to rural Ethiopia. Table 5 provides some of these common elements.

The survey samples two villages from each of the most populated regions. All villages depend on rain-fed agriculture. Four villages are in the highland areas and two villages are at lower altitudes. The central highlands (including parts of the Amhara and Oromo regions) are well suited for cereals and pulses, such as teff, barley, and horse beans. The farming system requires oxen to plow. Some southern highland areas are suitable for coffee (one such village, Gara Godo, is included in the survey), although coffee yields in this area are typically below the Ethiopian average. Both in 1989 and in 1994, yields were in fact close to zero in Gara Godo, mainly because of pests. The village of Adele Keke is located in the lowlands, and its farming system is based on sorghum, using hand-hoe technology. However, parts of the land in this village are well suited for chat production, and the good roads would help to establish it as a cash crop, since chat is highly perishable. Finally, the village of Domaa is a lowland village, founded as a (voluntary) resettlement area during the 1980s. The village depends on maize and other cereals, but it also grows enset, a permanent root crop forming the staple in specific parts of the South. Enset is also popular in Gara Godo.

Most households in Ethiopia are involved in agriculture. Very few households are without land (less than 4 percent). The land redistribution process, started in 1976, has been quite important in many of the communities in the study. About 25 percent of households in the sample report having lost some land during the land reform and subsequent continuous redistribution of the 1980s. In one village, Debre Berhan, the figure was as high as 40 percent of households; Domaa, the resettlement village, was least affected (less than 10 percent). Under the law, land could not be rented out or sold; households unable to farm the land (for example, because of illness or disability) were allowed to give the land to sharecropping; about a quarter of the sample are involved in sharecropping (for details, see Ayalew, Dercon, and Krishnan 1999).

Average landholdings vary between communities, reflecting local land pressure and farming systems. On average, each adult owns about half a hectare. Areas better suited for permanent crops, such as Adele Keke and Gara Godo, typically have lower landholdings. In two communities, Domaa and Korodegaga, some additional land was made available to households between 1989 and 1994. In Domaa, this land is newly cleared (this is a voluntary resettlement area that currently lacks water rather than land). In other areas, changes in household size and composition are responsible for changes to landholdings. In Korodegaga, more substantial land expansion took place as a result of the redistribution among farmers of the collective land owned until 1990 by the producer cooperative.[3] Other than in these two communities, changes in landholdings were quite limited from 1989 to 1994.

With one exception, all villages are close to small rural towns, but access to those towns is variable. The rural villages around the important town of Debre Berhan have straightforward access to the town. Domaa, on the other hand, is not far from a small town called Wacha; however, access is quite difficult. In the rainy season, for example, a river with no bridge has to be crossed, making the village regularly inaccessible for long periods of time. Dinki has similar problems of access. Although liberalization encourages more trade-oriented activities, differences in access to towns and villages may well dictate the extent of the benefit to households.

Table 6 gives the main sources of income, calculated from the 1994 income data. Crop agriculture is generally the largest source of income, although livestock is also very important in most areas. Most of the off-farm income derives from small businesses, usually food processing (including drinks), petty trading of agricultural products, or income from selling locally collected firewood and homemade charcoal. There is relatively little specialization in terms of activities in the villages; most households have many different income sources. Many of the off-farm activities (such as selling homemade drinks or dungcakes) are closely linked to agricultural activities.

The income and consumption data were not collected in a way that provides a full understanding of flow of own production into consumption over the seasons for both 1989 and 1994.[4] Still, the data reported in Table 7 suggest that a majority of households in the study communities

Table 6. Income Sources in 1994 as Percentages of Total Gross Income

		Village					
Item	Dinki	Debre Berhan	Adele Keke	Koro-degaga	Gara Godo	Domaa	Average
Crop agriculture	45	35	63	32	37	74	43
Livestock	31	40	10	39	21	10	32
Off farm	23	21	16	24	41	16	22
Transfers	1	1	11	5	1	0	3

Note: n = 358. The data give gross incomes, before deducting cash expenditure on inputs in agriculture and nonagriculture. Subsistence consumption of food is included in crop incomes, but not in livestock incomes. Although more details are available in 1994, the data definitions used allow as much comparability with the 1989 data as possible. Crop income includes land rental income (mainly from sharecropping). Live sales of animals are treated as part of livestock income, even though they may reflect asset portfolio transactions rather than returns to assets. Off-farm income includes business and wage income. It is likely to be an underestimate of actual gross income because of important seasonality in these activities, imperfectly accounted for in the survey. At the same time, input expenditure on these activities is expected to be higher and not accounted for using gross income measures. Finally, transfers include private remittances and gifts, but are mainly food aid and food-for-work incomes.
Source: Calculated from ERHS 1994.

are net buyers of basic food staples, especially in certain seasons. A rudimentary extrapolation and linking of the consumption and income data suggests that only 9 percent of households are net sellers across the villages, although this is likely to be a conservative estimate.[5] Still, more than a third of farmers sell food for cash—about 22 percent of their harvest, on average. Despite having virtually no households that are net sellers of food, Gara Godo had an estimated 80 percent of households that sold, on average, a third of their food harvest. In other words, they sell but also buy substantial amounts of food. Other results from the survey confirm that households rely on the market for food during certain times of the year, even for crops cultivated on the farm. On average, households reported that during about 10 weeks a year, they have no homegrown food in stock. During such a period, and if they can afford it, they will have to buy food from the market (or receive it as a gift). There is considerable variation within and across villages on this practice.

The fact that most of the households in the sample are likely to be net food buyers may have important implications for the welfare effects of the reform program. In particular, if reform raises the prices of basic staples, then a net seller will gain and a net buyer will lose from reform (Lipton

Table 7. Food Sales and Purchases

Item	Village						
	Dinki	Debre Berhan	Adele Keke	Koro-degaga	Gara Godo	Domaa	Average
Percent food deficit or surplus households							
Net food sellers	13	5	12	10	2	14	9
Neither buyers nor sellers	4	11	9	34	0	2	13
Sellers of any food	42	16	26	17	80	47	36
Average amount of food sold[a]	18	5	23	17	33	13	22
Number of weeks per year typically without homegrown food[b]							
Average	8	7	7	13	14	8	10
Up to 4	29	53	29	2	4	16	20
Up to 8	42	11	53	21	13	70	32
Up to 12	12	14	11	28	20	8	17
More	17	23	8	48	63	6	31

a. Percentage sold by those selling any food.
b. Average and frequency distribution in percent.
Source: ERHS 1994.

and Ravallion 1995). Table 7 raises the concern that if in some areas prices of basic staples rise as a result of market liberalization, then welfare losses may occur. In the analysis, this issue is complicated since the abolition of the quota system and other measures may have different general equilibrium effects on price and real income levels. The reduced seasonal price spread would also benefit households; however, disentangling the impact of seasonality in food sales and purchases is not possible. Finally, and probably most important, many households appear to grow and sell more expensive cereals (such as teff in Gara Godo) to buy cheaper food.

This study aims to understand changes in outcomes between 1989 and 1995 by trying the impact of economic reforms from other possible factors. So what happened in these villages during this period? Beyond the impact on prices and markets following the start of the economic reform program, a first possible factor is the end of the civil war. However, the civil war had relatively little effect on the communities, at least in terms of direct effects. With most of the fighting occurring in the northern part of Ethiopia, the village surveyed did not report any local fighting, destruction of property, or other direct effects from the war, with the exception of conscription (Dercon and Ayalew 1998; Webb, von Braun, and Yohannes 1992). Consequently, the direct effects of increased security, such as more opportunities for mobility toward local markets and lower price margins, are unlikely to have been very important. If anything, in one of the villages the security situation was probably worse after 1991 than before; Adele Keke experienced a period of uprising and repression of the OLF (Oromo Liberation Front), the erstwhile partner in the post-Mengistu government that launched a short-lived insurgency during 1992. Taxation during the latter part of the war was very high in some communities. Some households effectively paid 10 percent or more of their total income in such levies. Still, increased security across the country must have had important externalities on economic activities locally, even though it will be hard to identify the effects in the data.

Other changing conditions should also be taken into account when trying to explain outcomes. Rainfall is generally erratic in Ethiopia, but crucial for agricultural incomes. Table 8 gives details of the changes in rainfall during 1989 and 1994. Two measures for comparison are given for this period. First is the rainfall deviation from the mean (in percentages), in the 12 months preceding the main harvest relevant for the data of the survey. Consumption and the other welfare outcomes are, however, likely to be more sensitive to rainfall over several years, rather than just the previous year. A second measure is the rainfall in the five years preceding each survey round.[6] While 1994 was a good rainfall year for all but two communities (that is, all but two communities had above normal rains), it was better than 1989 for only two communities. National figures suggest that 1989 was a bad year for rainfall relative to 1994; however, in many southern and central areas there was a drought in 1993–94, as reflected in the data. The five-year average suggests that for Dinki and Gara Godo, the early 1990s had worse rainfall than in the second half of the 1980s. For Domaa and Adele Keke, the reverse was true. On average in the sample, the five-year average rainfall was slightly better in the 1990s than in the 1980s.

Few village-level characteristics changed in this period; for example, nongovernmental organization (NGO) activity remained similar. There

Table 8. Percentage of Rainfall, Relative to Mean

Time period	Dinki	Debre Berhan	Adele Keke	Koro-degaga	Gara Godo	Domaa
1989	18	9	–2	29	7	–5
1994	1	5	11	–27	–15	4
1985–89	5	–1	–12	–11	7	–6
1990–94	–6	–2	–1	–7	–7	6

Source: Rainfall data calculated from unpublished data supplied by the Meteorological Survey of Ethiopia.

was some improvement to the road in Gara Godo, even though it was not an all-weather road.

So what happened in terms of welfare outcomes in these villages? The welfare indicator used is food consumption data per adult equivalent in real terms (details and more descriptive statistics on alternative indicators are in Dercon and Krishnan 1998). No complete data on nonfood consumption were collected in 1989, so they are not reported.[7] Other welfare indicators, such as nutrition or health, were not available in 1989, so food consumption is our primary indicator. Food consumption is deflated by a food price deflator, using regional prices collected by the Central Statistical Authority.[8] Consumption is expressed in 1994 prices. Nutritional equivalence scales specific for East Africa were used to control for household size and composition. Since food consumption is unlikely to be characterized by economies of scale, no further scaling is used (Deaton 1997).

The questionnaire used during the survey collected consumption information based on a one-week recall of food consumption, from own sources, purchased, or from gifts. Seasonal analysis using the panel data covering 1994–95 revealed large seasonal fluctuations in consumption, presumably linked to price and labor demand fluctuations (Dercon and Krishnan 2000). We therefore tried to avoid welfare changes over time, which are caused by measuring food consumption during different seasons in both 1989 and 1994–95. To measure food consumption, the season used to collect data in 1989 was used again in 1994–95. More specifically, during the three rounds of the ERHS conducted in 1994–95, data were collected in three different seasons. For each household included in the 1989 to 1995 panel, we use only one observation from 1994–95, from the same season in which data were collected in 1989.[9] Table 9 gives the results.

Overall, we observe strong growth in mean food consumption in this period in this sample, the equivalent of about 9 percent per year. But there are substantial differences between villages.[10] In one village, mean food consumption seems to have declined, while in three other villages, growth is up more than 10 percent. Note that in four out of six cases, growth in food consumption is higher than the growth rate of private consumption per capita in the national accounts (table 1). It is also much higher than growth in agricultural GDP.[11]

It is interesting to look at what happened during 1989–95 to households at the lower end of the distribution of consumption across the sample. A simple and intuitive method is to identify the poor by using a poverty line and then observe the evolution of different poverty aggregates. The panel data also show poverty transitions during this period. To identify the poor, an absolute, nutrition-based poverty line is used. It will be fixed in real terms both intertemporally and spatially. The poverty line is an estimate of the cost of basic food needs (Ravallion 1994; Ravallion and Bidani 1994). The food needs are determined by considering the average diet of the lower half of the consumption distribution. This diet is then valued at local prices (using 1994 prices); in different areas in the sample, the value is in the

Table 9. Changes in Food Consumption per Month per Adult Equivalent between 1989 and 1994–95, in Birr and in 1994 Prices

| | | | Village | | | | |
Item	Dinki	Debre Berhan	Adele Keke	Koro-degaga	Gara Godo	Domaa	All
Mean food consumption 1989	50	53	64	37	27	25	42
Mean food consumption 1994	62	96	108	40	20	80	64
Yearly growth mean (percent)	4.3	12.4	11.1	1.5	-5.0	21.4	8.8

Note: n = 354.
Source: ERHS 1989 and 1994–95 surveys.

35–45 birr per month range.[12] This poverty line is applied to the real food consumption data. P-alpha poverty aggregates as used in Foster, Greer, and Thorbecke (1984) express different dimensions of poverty. In particular, the head count, the average normalized poverty gap, and the average squared poverty gap are presented. Table 10 gives the results.

Table 10. Poverty between 1989 and 1994–95

	Village						
Item	Dinki	Debre Berhan	Adele Keke	Koro-degaga	Gara Godo	Domaa	All
Head count 1989	0.42	0.34	0.42	0.73	0.80	0.86	0.61
Poverty gap 1989	0.14	0.12	0.10	0.39	0.46	0.45	0.29
Squared poverty gap 1989	0.07	0.05	0.05	0.25	0.30	0.27	0.17
Head count 1994–95	0.57	0.26	0.16	0.62	0.95	0.39	0.51
Poverty gap 1994–95	0.19	0.06	0.04	0.22	0.53	0.23	0.22
Squared poverty gap 1994–95	0.09	0.02	0.02	0.10	0.34	0.16	0.12
Percentage change 1989–95							
Head count	+36	−24	−61	−15	+18	−55	−16
Poverty gap	+32	−49	−60	−45	+15	−48	−26
Squared poverty gap	+32	−66	−62	−60	+13	−39	−31
Poverty elasticity at mean[a]							
Head count	1.53	−0.30	−0.88	−1.98	−0.68	−0.25	−0.30
Poverty gap	1.37	−0.62	−0.86	−5.82	−0.57	−0.22	−0.49
Squared poverty gap	1.33	−0.84	−0.90	−7.88	−0.47	−0.18	−0.59

Note: n = 358.
   a. The poverty elasticity is calculated as the ratio between the actual percentage change in poverty and the growth in mean consumption between 1989 and 1994–95.
   Source: Calculated from ERHS 1989 and 1994–95 survey data.

Overall, poverty fell between 1989 and 1994–95. The head count declined by 16 percent, and the other poverty measures by even more. The different experiences across villages are revealing: in four villages, we observed a substantial decline in poverty; in the two other villages, an increase in poverty.[13] Overall, poverty remains high, at about 50 percent. In five out of six villages population growth and poverty declines are inversely related, as one would expect. Finally, note that the poverty elasticities are typically relatively small, except for one village, where low growth appears to have coincided with substantial poverty declines. The overall poverty decreases across the sample are robust to the choice of the poverty line; in Dercon and Krishnan (1998) first-order welfare dominance was shown to exist for all reasonable poverty lines.

The figures in table 10 hide substantial poverty transitions in both directions. About 35 percent of the survey remained poor in both sample years; 26 percent moved out of poverty and about 16 percent moved into poverty during this period as well. Finally, the Gini coefficient moved in this period from 42.3 to 44.8. A decomposition of the total change in the head count into a growth and a redistribution effect (as in Datt and Ravallion 1992; Kakwani 1993a) showed that inequality increases made poverty higher by 3.1 percentage points, but food consumption growth brought poverty down by 13.2 percentage points. In conclusion, food consumption growth was relatively high in these villages and poverty declined considerably, although the poverty elasticity appears generally low. Inequality increases, movements into poverty, and differing experiences across communities in this period suggest that growth did not affect all households in the same way. Differential impact of the reforms is a possible explanation, but their different exposure to weather and other shocks is also a plausible one.

NOTES

1. All communities appear to have suffered during the 1980s from drought and hunger. In one village, Debre Berhan, the response was limited to selling livestock and cutting back food intake. In the other villages, wild foods consumption and the sale of other assets came into play. A fifth of households in Korodegaga migrated in search of income and food; about a quarter of households went to a feeding camp. In all, more than 40 percent of households

received food aid in this period (more details in Webb, von Braun, and Yohannes 1992).

2. The ERHS covers 15 villages and 1,477 households, including 6 villages and 362 households covered by the 1989 survey. The ERHS is a panel data survey and data on the same 1,477 households were collected in 1994 and in several more rounds. By design, it is also a panel data set starting in 1989 for 362 of these households, a subsample of the ERHS sample. This subsample forms the basis of the current text.

3. By 1994, 4.5 percent of the sample were no longer landless.

4. This is a standard problem with one-round data collection per year. Harvest data and other income sources are based on recall related to the main seasons (up to 12 months ago), while consumption is measured using a short recall period close to the interview. Corrections for seasonal dimensions in consumption and income generation are possible, but are often conducted in an ad hoc fashion. Comparability in the questionnaire design between the different rounds was high for the consumption modules but less so for the production side.

5. It assumes that in every week of the year, the household buys the same proportion of its total food staples consumption (pulses, cereals, and tubers) from the market as in the week of consumption data collection. A net seller is then a farmer who sold more cereals, pulses, and tubers (as reported relative to all the harvests in the last 12 months) than the extrapolated total consumption from the market. Given that much data collection was not done in a post-harvest period, this is likely to be an underestimate of the net sellers. Furthermore, there is no clear account included in this calculation of the food used in simple food processing, such as making njera or drinks for the market, which contributes substantially to household income.

6. In general, the data are unlikely to be precise for average levels, since only data over time from the nearest rainfall station were available. However, it is likely that local rainfall variability may be well measured by these data.

7. Also, since these households are relatively poor, food shares are very high—on average 78 percent in 1994–95—so food consumption is likely to be a good indication of overall consumption.

8. Local prices were collected in 1994–95 as well, but to increase consistency of the results, we used the same source for both 1989 and 1994–95, that is, the Ethiopian Central Statistical Authority.

9. To be more precise, the data from round one to three of the panel data survey were collected over an 18-month period, each round in a different season. Logistical considerations meant that data in each site were not necessarily in the same month as in other sites. Consequently, for the comparison between 1989 and 1994–95, the data for two villages are from the first round of 1994, for two villages from the second round of 1994, and for two villages from

1995; consequently, we refer to a comparison as between 1989 and 1994–95. Details and implications are in Dercon and Krishnan (1998).

10. There is no reason that in practice consumption would have grown each year by a similar rate in this period. If anything, all evidence on rural Ethiopia, including from the national accounts, suggests very large yearly fluctuations, which are only partially smoothed (Dercon and Krishnan 2000).

11. Although this is not the subject matter of the current paper, data are by now also available for subsequent years, and a few comments help to put the earlier evolution into context. Overall, further growth in food consumption took place. One village, Domaa, lost some of its recovery, while mean consumption declined substantially in Dinki, which is consistent with findings of growing deprivation in other data reported in this section. Gara Godo experienced a substantial recovery, aided by growth in coffee earnings, while the other villages grew even faster than before. These growth rates are substantial, but of course, earlier food consumption levels were extremely low. In short, the increases between 1989 and 1995, while fragile, were not reversed in this period.

12. In 1994 dollars, this meant about US$7.00 per month per adult. Even using a typical PPP-deflator of about a third, this is still well below the $1.00 per day norm.

13. In Dercon and Krishnan (1998), significant levels of these poverty changes have been reported, following Kakwani (1993b). The overall declines and the changes in four out of six villages were significant at 5 percent or less.

CHAPTER 4

Economic Reform and the Village Economy

iven the relative importance of crop agriculture in the local economy, the evolution of producer prices relative to overall consumer price inflation provides a useful starting point for the analysis of the reforms' impact. Table 11 gives the average increase in producer prices in each of the communities relative to the consumer price evolution. It can be read as the percentage movement in terms of trade, using 1989 terms of trade between producer and consumer goods as a base. The percentage change of the average real producer prices per community for all crops, as well as for subgroups, is reported.[1] Since the reforms generally provide increased incentives for tradable commodities, it is of interest to distinguish them from the price evolution in nontradables. Like most African countries, there is relatively little large-scale international private food trade taking place in Ethiopia (even if the markets did become liberalized); however, there is a very active market in most food crops, especially cereals. Internal market liberalization provides further incentives for trade in these commodities. From the point of view of the village economy, it would appear appropriate to include those actively traded commodities as tradables. Nontradables include commodities rarely moved across any large distances, mainly because of high transaction costs due to a low value in relation to weight and volume. In the data, these include root crops such as enset and sweet potatoes. Finally, table 11 also reports the relative price movement of the crops that were liable to be designated

Table 11. Real Producer Prices: Percentage Increases Relative to 1989

			Village				
Item	Dinki	Debre Berhan	Adele Keke	Koro-degaga	Gara Godo	Domaa	Average
All crops	+28	+21	+12	+65	−37	+35	+26
Quota crops[a]	+29	+20	+15	+74	−22		
Tradables[b]	+28	+23	+15	+65	−12	+49	+31
Nontradables[c]			−38		−77	−23	
Food	+31	+21	+25	+65	−37	+35	+28
Coffee					+49		
Chat			−9				

Note: Percentage changes in terms of trade, based on the movement of producer prices relative to consumption price inflation. The producer prices for different crops are weighted using the contribution to total crop income in 1994 of each crop (including production for home consumption). The reported figures are based on the producer price indexes, averaged across households in each community and across the sample. Producer prices for all indexes were taken from publications on rural producer prices at the subregional level, collected by the Central Statistical Authority. To achieve maximum comparability, only consumer prices collected by the Central Statistical Authority were used as well. Data were compiled for the same months so that differences do not reflect seasonality. Blank spaces signify that particular crops are not grown in this village. Averages are calculated only if all villages grow the crops.
    a. Quota crops: only using crops for which a quota had to be sold to the AMC.
    b. Tradables: regularly traded food and cash crops in Ethiopia, that is, most cereals and cash crops.
    c. Nontradables: crops such as enset and sweet potatoes.
    Source: ERHS and Central Statistical Authority.

quotas in each community. The abolition of the quota system probably had an additional effect on prices.

The observed producer price changes are generally consistent with the earlier predictions. The abolition of the quota system and new market reforms appear to have resulted in increases in real producer prices, which have increased, on average, about 26 percent. The increases are higher for those crops included in the quota system compared to other crops typically traded. As previously discussed, the effect on prices of the quota system's abolition is ambiguous, although surplus areas are likely to have benefited from the liberalization of regional trade. The national evidence pointed to higher producer prices in surplus areas. Quota crops were generally selected on the basis of predicted surpluses, and the results in table 11 are consistent with this pattern. After liberalization, incentives for nontradable crops strongly decreased, which is in line with an increased market orientation.

In Gara Godo, however, prices moved quite differently. It is located in a densely populated area, with a network of relatively good roads, and liberalization appears to have brought down producer prices. The decline is less steep for the main cereal crops relative to nontradables, but it is still substantial. Terms of trade for coffee, traditionally an important cash crop in the area, moved very favorably, partly because of the coffee boom of 1994–95, but also because of the devaluation. This favorable price increase is not reflected in the real incomes of the households in the sample, however, because there was a coffee harvest failure in 1994, brought about by pests and a drought that occurred at a crucial point in the growth cycle.[2]

Finally, chat, another important export crop in Ethiopia, is quite successful in Adele Keke, but its terms of trade actually fell in the period 1989–94. Because chat was rarely traded via the official channels, its price generally reflected the black market exchange rate; therefore, the devaluation has had little impact. Increased production and reduced rents from smuggling may well have depressed the prices. Still, during the period 1989–94, chat prices in real terms stood at about three times the level of the early 1980s.

The fact that most households are net buyers of food does not mean that they will be disadvantaged by crop price increases. The reported crop producer price increases are relative to a food cost-of-living index, so these food crop price increases still result in real income gains.[3] Many households sell some of their crops or use crops to process food for sale, and they buy different food products at different times. Better producer prices increase their purchasing power, even if they choose not to sell the food they produce but to consume it themselves. Since seasonal fluctuations appear to have decreased, this real income increase is underestimated using only the average producer price.

A central question in much of the debate about the effects of market reform and increased incentives is whether farm households are actually responding to the changes in real producer prices. Table 12 provides some descriptive evidence on this debate. Recall that households have access to land that is strictly controlled, since private ownership of land is nonexistent. Consequently, any response to increased prices must come from either a reallocation of land or increases in factor intensity and productivity. Table 12 lists the percentage of total cultivated land area that has been diverted away from the crops that farm households had to supply as part of the quota system. Although table 11 shows that prices for these quota crops had also increased substantially, households switched away from those crops nonetheless. This shift shows that the quota system was inefficient: it forced farmers to allocate land suboptimally.[4]

The area allocated to nontradable crops, such as enset and sweet potatoes, expanded in Adele Keke and in Gara Godo. However, this expansion is mainly due to the increase of permanent crops such as coffee, since enset is typically suitable for intercropping (that is, plots are planted with different crops at the same time) with permanent crops. The large decline in land allocated to nontradables in Domaa (where none of the permanent crops are grown) is consistent with the evolution of relative prices. Finally, we also observe an important increase in export crop allocation in those areas well suited for growing these crops. In Gara Godo and Adele Keke, the area was expanded by about 5 to 10 percent of total land area cultivated, by increasing coffee trees and chat bushes.[5] The increase in permanent crops is especially impressive in Adele Keke, where a large number of new chat bushes were planted.

Table 12. Selected Changes in Land Allocation, 1989–94

	Village					
Item	Dinki	Debre Berhan	Adele Keke	Koro-degaga	Gara Godo	Domaa
Change in land allocation to quota crops[a]	–12%	–7%	–9%	–11%	–21%	
Increase in land allocated to nontradables			2%		2%	–6%
Increase in land allocated to cash crops	2%		10%		5%	
Increase in number of trees/bushes of chat and coffee (average per farm)[b]			256 (767)		8 (47)	

Note: Blank spaces signify that particular crops are not grown in this village.

a. Percentage change in total land allocated in the village to crops subject to quotas until 1988.

b. Average increase per farm; mean holding in 1994 in parentheses. No data on replacement of old trees/bushes. Data for Adele Keke are for chat; data for Gara Godo are for coffee.

Table 13 elaborates on this issue of the export crop expansion during the period of reforms. It gives data on the percentage of expanding households as well as the mean expansion per farm in the village, by period. It is striking that the coffee expansion in Gara Godo picked up again in recent years, after the devaluation. But the largest expansion occurred after the start of the coffee boom in 1994; it is hard to claim, on the basis of this evidence, that this expansion is due to the reforms,[6] but better prices (and possibly inflated expectations) seem to result in a positive supply response. Chat expansion in Adele Keke also follows an interesting pattern. Much of the expansion took place before the devaluation, reflecting both the status of chat as a prime smuggling crop and its massive price increase during the 1980s. But the expansion continued after the devaluation. Chat expansion now seems past its prime, with little expansion in recent years; however, in the mid-1990s, about 88 percent of households were growing the crop. In short, both villages, Gara Godo and Adele Keke, illustrate that farmers appear to respond to increased real prices, but large-scale smuggling before the reforms and the coffee boom limit the extent to which the observed pattern is a direct effect of the devaluation. However, by offering better prices through official channels, the reforms make it less likely that the investments in permanent crops will become quickly unprofitable and possibly reversed if smuggling is repressed and the coffee boom comes to an end.

While real producer prices have increased in most villages, input prices have also increased. Higher prices for fertilizer were accompanied by

Table 13. Export Crop Expansion, 1983–95

	Village			
	Adele Keke (chat)		Gara Godo (coffee)	
Time period	Percentage of households expanding	Mean expansion of bushes (all households)[a]	Percentage of households expanding	Mean expansion of trees (all households)[a]
1983–88	39	90	28	4
1989–91	50	116	14	1
1992–93	71	132	16	3
1994	8	9	76	5

a. Mean expansion is the total number of bushes or trees planted per household in the village.
Source: Calculated from survey data from ERHS 1994.

much higher availability. In general, producer prices appear to have increased by more than fertilizer prices, partly because of continuing subsidies during 1989–94. Locally, prices faced by farmers may well have increased because of changing credit supply conditions. Although we do not have systematic evidence comparing fertilizer prices over time at the farmgate level in the study villages, the available evidence implies higher increases than the national data suggest. Data on input intensity were not available in 1989, but table 14 reports some more qualitative data on changes in fertilizer use in this period.

About half the sample used fertilizer in 1994, but with a very wide variation across villages. Note that this is not just due to differences in farming systems, since all areas grow cereals or other crops that would benefit from fertilizer in terms of expected yield. On average, 43 percent had not changed the amounts of fertilizer used relative to 1989, while 31 percent used less, despite higher availability. In some communities, the decline in application rates is striking; for example, in Debre Berhan, a village where fertilizer use was typically widespread, about half the households decreased the quantities applied. In Domaa, fertilizer use is still virtually zero. These figures are consistent with the finding that reform in fertilizer markets did not result in a strong increase in fertilizer use. As a result, there were large unsold stocks of fertilizer by 1995.[7] Other quali-

Table 14. Evolution in Fertilizer Use, 1989–94
(percent)

			Village				
Item	Dinki	Debre Berhan	Adele Keke	Koro-degaga	Gara Godo	Domaa	Average
Fertilizer used in 1994	9	92	58	59	91	0	54
Used more than in 1989[a]	0	27	33	56	4	n.a.	25
Same as in 1989[a]	33	25	54	44	58	n.a.	43
Less than in 1989[a]	67	47	13	0	38	n.a.	31

n.a. Not applicable.
a. Only for those who are using fertilizer in 1994 and did so in 1989.

tative evidence from the survey points to the relatively high cost of fertilizer as a particular problem; in our sample 86 percent of those using less fertilizer claimed that the fertilizer was too expensive. About 65 percent of those households not using any modern inputs similarly reported that they did not acquire them because of their cost.[8]

Thus far, the focus of this text has been on the reforms and their effect on crop agriculture only. As shown in table 6, other income sources are also important. The move to a more market-oriented economic policy and increased security after 1991 may well have contributed positively to activities such as sales of livestock products, trade of other commodities, small-scale business activities, or temporary migration for wage labor. Table 15 presents evidence that in this period, more households became involved in off-farm activities. The table orders the activities on the basis of broad groups of entry-barriers, in the form of skills or capital requirements. The first group participates in gathering and collecting activities, like firewood collection and dungcake sales; little investment and skill are needed. The second group is centered around crafts or petty trading, which involve some entry barriers, usually in the form of some basic investment for weaving, spinning, or acquiring a basic stock of commodities for trade. The third group is made up of people with more skills, such as builders or carpenters. The fourth group, wage employment, is also listed; this category includes wage labor but is mainly casual labor, often in urban areas. This last category typically includes jobs that are better paying than the other three groups.[9] Table 15 shows that for virtually all activities, there has been an expansion. The expansion is greatest for casual wage labor and especially crafts for sale and trading. There is also a move away from basic gathering activities to activities requiring more investment and skill.

Table 16 presents some indication of what these different changes and responses may have meant for incomes and their structure in the sample. While the data are far from perfect for detailed comparisons over time, they confirm the patterns of consumption increases, activity changes, and relative price movements. In four out of six villages, real income from crops increased, which is in line with increases in real producer prices. Gara Godo experienced both falling crop terms of trade and harvest failure for enset and coffee, while Dinki had a total failure of the short rains.

Table 15. Involvement in Off-Farm Activities: Percentage of Households Reporting to Be Involved

	Village						
Year/activity	Dinki	Debre Berhan	Adele Keke	Koro-degaga	Gara Godo	Domaa	Average
1989							
Gathering/ collecting for sale[a]	0	92	28	49	36	0	37
Crafts and trade[b]	23	5	0	0	38	2	10
Builder, carpentry, other skilled	4	10	9	1	20	4	7
Wage employment (cash)	4	15	11	0	13	0	7
1994							
Gathering/ collecting for sale[a]	2	98	7	94	0	0	40
Crafts and trade[b]	66	19	23	84	78	56	56
Builder, carpentry, other skilled	9	15	7	4	20	12	10
Wage employment (cash)	28	19	37	16	27	33	26

a. Includes firewood collection and sale and making charcoal.
b. Includes weaving, spinning, petty food trade, food processing for sale, and other activities.
Source: Calculated from survey data.

Livestock income (including live sales) increased considerably overall, but this is dominated by strong increases in at least two villages. Wage and business income increased more evenly and considerably. On average, real incomes went up in line with consumption (table 9). Overall growth rates were highest in off-farm activities and in livestock. This is striking, since most of the reforms were primarily focused on crop agriculture. Since many off-farm activities are linked to agriculture (such as food processing or petty trade in crops), this should not be surprising. Nevertheless, the largest gains for the rural economy of the reform program may have been the increased market-oriented opportunities, which allowed households to move into higher returns from off-farm activities, away from gathering and collecting activities. Real consumption grew fastest in areas with strong gains in crop incomes between 1989 and 1994 (Adele Keke and Domaa).

The large growth in livestock income is remarkable and justifies some further attention. The largest part of livestock income comes from live sales of livestock—mostly goats, sheep, and cattle. As in other surveys, constructing household income accounts for mixed farming households is complicated. Regarding livestock, some of the sales of livestock may be a genuine return to their stock while other sales may be part of dissaving (that is, drawing down savings) to smooth consumption in the face of

Table 16. Real Incomes per Year per Adult, in Birr and in 1994 Prices

Year/ activity	Village							Increase (percent per year)
	Dinki	Debre Berhan	Adele Keke	Koro-degaga	Gara Godo	Domaa	Average	
1989								
Crop and land	290	279	163	64	99	70	157	
Livestock	23	285	77	23	9	49	79	
Wage and business	32	84	118	86	28	1	60	
Transfers	13	10	18	3	15	22	12	
Total	381	659	413	176	166	144	320	
1994								
Crop and land	137	290	277	169	58	220	190	3.9
Livestock	98	370	46	208	34	30	145	12.9
Wage and business	72	172	70	128	65	46	98	10.1
Transfers	4	4	47	25	2	1	14	2.2
Total	311	837	440	531	159	297	447	6.9

Source: Calculated from ERHS 1989 and 1994 surveys.

low, unexpected, or expected income draws. The fast increase in the share of income from livestock in Dinki or Gara Godo, for example, gives some indication that these households may have been dissaving. The evolution of asset data in this period may clarify this; table 17 gives details on all tradable assets owned by the household. Values are deflated by consumer prices and expressed in 1994 values per adult equivalent. Livestock is by far the most important asset, so the discussion will be confined to changes in livestock over this period.

Table 17. Asset Values and Changes, 1989–94

	Village						
Item	Dinki	Debre Berhan	Adele Keke	Koro-degaga	Gara Godo	Domaa	Average
Nonfarm assets in 1989[a]	20	108	21	10	5	7	29
Nonfarm assets in 1994[a]	20	51	23	29	3	10	24
Farm assets in 1989[b]	13	27	6	9	4	9	12
Farm assets in 1994[b]	14	20	5	10	2	3	10
Livestock in 1989	466	1592	132	175	97	3	425
Livestock in 1994	283	1396	197	432	63	152	452
Percentage owning livestock in 1989	82	98	60	40	46	6	55
Percentage owning livestock in 1994	75	100	84	98	73	78	86
Livestock units in 1989[c]	0.43	1.53	0.13	0.18	0.11	0.01	0.41
Livestock units in 1994[c]	0.39	1.55	0.27	0.65	0.14	0.31	0.59

		Village					
Item	Dinki	Debre Berhan	Adele Keke	Koro-degaga	Gara Godo	Domaa	Average
Livestock annual growth (values)	–10	–3	8	20	–8	114	1
Livestock annual growth (units)	–2	0	16	30	5	122	8
Annual growth, all assets	–9	–3	7	19	–9	54	1
Percentage of households selling livestock during crisis in 1980s[d]	79	92	9	38	87	59	61
Percentage herd sold[e]	28	13	8	40	67	92	39
Index livestock units in 1994 (precrisis = 100)[f]	65	88	191	219	41	453	87
Index livestock values in 1994 (precrisis = 100)[g]	43	76	138	148	21	380	64

Note: All values expressed in 1994 prices (deflated by the within-survey consumer price index) and in per adult equivalent.

a. Nonfarm assets: furniture, utensils, jewelry, etc.

b. Farm assets: ploughs, carts, tools, etc.

c. Livestock units: based on average national relative prices, from CSA-sources. Oxen, mules = 1; horses, camels = 0.5; bull = 0.75, cow = 0.70, calf = 0.30, heifer = 0.4; sheep, goat = 0.1.

d. Households were asked whether they sold livestock to cope with the crisis years around the mid-1980s and how much it raised.

e. A rough estimate of the percentage of the herd sold in value terms, assuming that the precrisis herd was equal to the value in 1989 plus the reported crisis sales.

f. This index puts the estimated precrisis herd at 100, and assuming that the 1989 herd index value is equal to the precrisis herd minus the crisis sales. The 1994 index value is then calculated using the actual growth rates in the livestock herd reported above in the table. Calculations in equivalent units. The same household was defined as having at least one or more members of the household living at the same place and cultivating some of the same land as in the mid-1980s.

g. The same as in f, but now using livestock values. Note that calculations assume zero livestock price inflation in the 1980s. Note that general inflation after 1985 remained relatively low, while livestock prices had fallen considerably during the famine. This latter is bound to have resulted in an underestimate of livestock herd values in the mid-1980s, so that in real 1994 prices, the recovery may have been lower.

On average, there was little growth in the value of livestock herds, about 1 percent per year during 1989–94. This number obscures a few important facts. First, the percentage of livestock owners increased from 55 to 86 percent during this period. The average declines are mainly due to declines in Debre Berhan and Dinki, where livestock herds are typically larger. In two other villages, Korodegaga and Domaa, there was a large expansion. Second, the small increase in average herd values can be attributed to lower price increases for livestock, compared to general consumer price inflation. In the sample villages, livestock prices increased by 30 to 59 percent (on average, 39 percent), well below consumer price increases in this period. This is reflected in the livestock data expressed in terms of equivalent units, a standard weighted measure of the herd size. On average, herds grew everywhere by 8 percent per year. Still, herds stagnated in Debre Berhan and went down in Dinki; a very large expansion took place in Korodegaga and Domaa.

Linking these data with the income data clarifies to some extent the changes in livestock incomes during this period. Higher livestock incomes in Gara Godo and especially in Dinki appear mainly due to dissavings; herd values fell considerably in those villages. In both villages, livestock sales coincided with much lower harvests than before. In Korodegaga, higher livestock income shares reflect a large expansion of the herd. Here, sales are comparable to cashing in on asset value accumulation. Finally, large increases in crop incomes in both Adele Keke and Domaa coincided with the accumulation of livestock herds.

Finally, the data allow some inference on the long-term livestock evolution in these villages. Since livestock is by far the most important tradable asset in the rural economy, this gives some idea of the long-term wealth evolution since the mid-1980s. Data were collected on distress sales of livestock during the crisis affecting the communities in the mid-1980s. Linking the values of these sales to livestock values in 1989 and 1994 provides compelling evidence that, on average, these communities had by 1994 barely recovered from those crises. In particular, livestock herd sizes are still below the levels of the mid-1980s. In value terms, because of the relative decline in livestock prices, herds are worth only about two-thirds of their mid-1980s value. In two villages, Dinki and Gara Godo, herd sizes have fallen considerably compared to the mid-1980s. In these two towns, food consumption growth has also lagged and real incomes appear to have declined as well. These communities clearly have not recovered at all and, in fact, appear to have slipped further downhill. In Adele Keke, Korodegaga, and Domaa, herds have grown considerably, well beyond precrisis levels. As these villages attest, periods of change affect different communities in different ways, not just with respect to consumption levels, but also with respect to asset levels.

NOTES

1. Data used are for 1989 and for 1994. It could be argued that these may be exceptional years, which implies that these price changes do not reflect genuine permanent movements, but rather transitory differences. A systematic comparison for longer periods was not feasible because of gaps in the data between 1990 and 1993, while the Census of 1994–95 stopped producer price data collection until late 1995. Still, an inspection of the available data suggests that the change is systematic and took effect at least after 1992. It also means that the usual problem of expectations and lag structure when analyzing supply response is of less relevance.

2. Later rounds of the panel survey in subsequent years not used in this text have shown an important recovery in coffee output in this area.

3. To allow intertemporal as well as interregional comparisons, a general national (or cross-community) basket was used to construct the weights in the consumer price deflator, although some sensitivity analysis was performed. It may be argued that local baskets would have been better for understanding changing relative incentives for agricultural production. As it turned out, using area-specific consumption baskets made the real producer price increases even larger, so that the interpretation is not affected.

4. As was argued before, if markets had been functioning perfectly, the quota system would have been equivalent to a lump-sum tax and would not have had implications for production by agricultural households, since they could have bought the quota from the market using the revenue from other crops or activities. Consequently, since we observe a switch away from these crops, growing other crops for sale and then buying the quota crop in the market is unlikely to have been a profitable option for farmers, for example, because of transaction costs in the crop market.

5. Even in Dinki, where only a small part of the land near a river is suitable for cultivating coffee, an important expansion took place. Since coffee and chat take several years to reach full production, this expansion is not yet reflected in harvests included in the 1994 data.

6. The average number of coffee trees is relatively small in Gara Godo in comparison with the main coffee-growing areas. In this village, 94 percent of farm households currently grow coffee.

7. Other data have suggested that, in other areas in Ethiopia, fertilizer application rates have increased in this period. For example, in 10 other villages (about 900 households) studied as part of the ERHS (1994), only 7 percent of farmers had reduced application rates, and 30 percent had actually increased usage. Contrary to the sample used in this paper, these villages include many more "high potential" areas, which may be able to take advantage of modern inputs and generally benefit from better extension and input delivery.

8. Note that one must be careful in the interpretation of this response: it does not need to mean that no profits could be made from applying (more) fertilizer, even at current prices; there is evidence from simulation studies that it appears generally still profitable (Mulat, Said, and Jayne 1997). However, it could point to problems with working capital constraints and input credit supply, or problems with inefficient use related to skills and information issues.

9. Because of differences in questionnaire design and the detail of questions, comparing the data from the two rounds could be done using these admittedly imperfect categories.

PART 2

Explaining Growth and Poverty Changes

Methodology for Decomposing Growth and Poverty Changes

The panel data available provide facts on changes in welfare and poverty over time.[1] In this chapter a framework will be used to assess these changes in welfare and to what extent they can be attributed to the economic reforms, rather than, say, climatic conditions or idiosyncratic shocks faced by households. Reforms affect household incomes and consumption by changing the prices and wages in the economy. Households may also be affected by changes in availability of public goods or direct transfers. The available data show that there is little evidence of changes in transfers or public goods during 1989–95, so it will not be a consideration in the econometric analysis.

DECOMPOSING INCOME

Household net incomes can be seen as total returns on the different assets and endowments the household owns or has access to. Assets and endowments include land, labor, human capital, and local endowments, such as agricultural potential and infrastructure. These assets are applied to a diversified portfolio of activities, possibly with some other inputs, such as fertilizer in agriculture or string to tie firewood before sale. Most activities are business activities—running a farm or off-farm activities that have close links to the farm, such as making and selling local beer or livestock products. Virtually all households in the sample have access to some land.

Relatively little income is derived from wages or transfers; at the same time, little labor tends to be hired in or out, and land sales are prohibited. To simplify the analysis, think of the household trying to allocate some fixed (for example, land, labor) and variable inputs (for example, fertilizer) to produce output (for example, crops or beer) and profit. The fixed inputs coincide with the household's endowments (such as land, land quality, labor, or human capital) and their presence is equivalent to assuming missing markets for these production factors, while some inputs such as fertilizer or seeds are bought.

This approach assumes that different household activities, including nonfarm and farm activities, can be considered as producing some composite good. In agricultural economic analysis, this approach is not uncommon when considering total farm output. Here, it is applied to all household income-generating activities.

To separate out the effects of changing relative prices in the economy as part of the reform program, the profit function approach is used; a simple underlying production function represents the household's allocation of inputs (De Janvry, Sadoulet, and Fafchamps 1991; Singh, Squire, and Strauss 1986). The panel data provides variation in prices so that price responsiveness can be estimated. Also, since good data on all output and income sources are not available, estimating a profit function still allows us to make inferences on the overall effects of the economic reforms. At the same time, heterogeneity across households can be addressed via panel data, at least under certain assumptions about the form of heterogeneity.

Let the household's joint income generation process be described by $q = g(x, k, u)$, in which q is total output, x is a vector of n variable inputs, k is a vector of j fixed inputs, and u is a vector of m stochastic factors, such as agroclimatic conditions. Risk is introduced as a factor in the production function. The household is assumed to maximize profits from its activities,[2] which can be simply written as

(1)
$$\max_{x} Y = p \cdot g(x, k, u) - p^x x$$

in which p is the output price and p^x are input prices.

The optimal x can be substituted back into the objective function to define the profit function Y as a function of input and output prices, fixed factors, and exogenous shocks. If one assumes that the production function takes on the Cobb-Douglas form, that is, $q = a \cdot x^\alpha k^\beta u^\gamma$, then straightforward manipulation yields a profit function, defined as

(2)
$$Y = a^{\frac{1}{1-\alpha}} \cdot \alpha^{\frac{1}{1-\alpha}} \cdot (1-\alpha) \cdot k^{\frac{\beta}{1-\alpha}} \cdot p^{\frac{1}{1-\alpha}} p^{x\frac{-\alpha}{1-\alpha}} u^{\frac{\gamma}{1-\alpha}}.$$

Using logarithms, a useful form for empirical analysis emerges as

(3)
$$\ln Y = \ln a^* + \frac{1}{1 - \sum_n \alpha_n} \ln p + \sum_n \frac{-\alpha_n}{1 - \sum_n \alpha_n} \ln p_n^x + \sum_j \frac{\beta_j}{1 - \sum_n \alpha_n} \ln k_j + \sum_m \frac{\gamma_m}{1 - \sum_n \alpha_n} \ln u_m$$

$$\text{with } \ln a^* = \frac{1}{1 - \sum_n \alpha_n} \ln a + \sum_n \frac{\alpha_n}{1 - \sum_n \alpha_n} \ln \alpha_n + \ln\left(1 - \sum_n \alpha_n\right).$$

For further manipulation, using subscript i to denote different households, and introducing a household-specific effect, δ_i, for each household i, equation 3 can be written as

(4) $\ln Y_i = \delta_i + \ln a_i^* + \varphi^* \ln p_i + \sum_n \alpha_n^* \ln p_m^x + \sum_j \beta_j^* \ln k_{ij} + \sum_m \gamma_m^* \ln u_{im}.$

When comparing incomes over time after a period of reform, a number of elements in equation 4 may change. First, reform is likely to affect input and output prices, which in turn affects household incomes. Second, households may have expanded or reduced some of their fixed inputs; for example, the available labor or human capital may have changed. Third, the reforms may have encouraged changes in the production. More realistically, since the model assumes the production of one composite commodity, relative output and input price changes may have induced a shift in the optimal portfolio of activities, implying some changes in the optimal technology used (such as more intensive in some variable or fixed production factors).[3] Finally, the shock variables are likely to take on different values. Allowing for these different changes, considering periods t and $t + 1$ as before and after the reforms, respectively, and denoting Δ as the difference in values between $t + 1$ and t, differences in profits over time can be defined as

$$\Delta \ln Y_i = \Delta \ln a_i^* + \varphi_{t+1}^* \Delta \ln p_i + \Delta \varphi^* \ln p_{it} + \sum_u \alpha_{nt+1}^* \Delta \ln p_{in}^x + \sum_n \Delta \alpha_n^* \ln p_{int}^x$$

(5)

$$+ \sum_j \beta_{jt+1}^* \Delta \ln k_{ij} + \sum_j \Delta \beta_j^* \ln k_{ijt} + \sum_m \gamma_{mt+1}^* \Delta \ln u_{im} + \sum_m \Delta \gamma_m^* \ln u_{imt}.$$

Introducing an error term and estimating equation 5 provide estimates of the different elasticities relative to prices and changes in fixed inputs, and it controls for heterogeneity in the form of household fixed effects. At the same time, an estimate is obtained for any changes in those elasticities over time that are due to shifts in the underlying technology of combining inputs. Equation 5 distinguishes the effects of changing prices from changes in the household endowments and from shocks faced by the household. Provided that price changes can be linked to the reform program, any observed changing income levels can be assessed regarding any link to the reforms. A simple way to present these results is to use the estimates from equation 5 and calculate the contribution of each of these factors to explain mean income changes; this method is similar to a Oaxaca-Blinder decomposition (Blinder 1973; Oaxaca 1973). In particular, equation 5 can be summed for all i, and each term can then be divided by the sum of changes in log incomes. When equation 5 is estimated using a method in which the expected error term is zero (such as ordinary least squares, OLS), an exact decomposition is possible.

LINKING POVERTY AND GROWTH: SIMULATING THE IMPACT OF VARIABLES

The analysis described above allows us to see how different factors contribute to changes in the mean real income levels. However, in this text, our real concern is how different observed factors contribute to the change in poverty over time. This is not self-evident. A poverty index is generally not a linear function of real incomes; consequently, changes in real incomes are not linearly related to changes in poverty. For example, the poverty gap index is, for each poor individual, linear in real incomes but nonlinear as an aggregate measure. When considering changes over time with regard to particular factors, the group of poor and nonpoor may change as well, so there is no simple, exact way to link the effects of growth to the effects on poverty.[4] The standard approach for studying the effects of changes over time of particular factors on poverty is to construct the counterfactual real income distribution (via microsimulations) and then to calculate the difference in the poverty indicator between the original and the counterfactual distribution. (In chapter 6, we will use this approach to investigate the specific individual contributions of different factors on the changes in poverty during the period under consideration, 1989–95.)

However, it is possible to derive a simple analytical result that *describes* the calculations one implements during such a microsimulation exercise, given the questions asked in this paper; in principle, *any* counterfactual can be simulated and its impact assessed on any poverty index. However, suppose our interest is to investigate specific variables and how they affect poverty changes and explain growth? Since equation 5 considers changes in the natural logarithm of income, we can use a poverty index that is defined in log income as well. Furthermore, we can consider an additive separable poverty index, which for each poor person is linear in log incomes. The normalized poverty gap, defined over the log of income as the underlying household welfare measure, satisfies this property.[5]

Formally denote $\ln Y_{it}$ as y_{it}; z as the log of the poverty line; q_t as the number of people falling below the poverty line in the current period; and n as the total number of individuals who are all observed over time.[6] If all individuals are ordered from poor to rich in each period, then this measure can be defined as

(6)
$$P_t = \frac{1}{n} \sum_{i=1}^{q_t} \frac{z - y_{it}}{z}.$$

Let's consider two periods of time, 0 and 1, and introduce a specific counterfactual, in which the change of income over time is equal to X_i. For example, this could be the change in real income stemming from the actual change in one of the fixed endowments in equation 5, or $X_i = \beta^*_{jt+1} \Delta \ln k_{ij}$. It is then possible to calculate the counterfactual real income for person i, y_{i1}^*, as

(7)
$$y_{i1}^* = y_{i0} + X_i.$$

Given this change in income for each i between the two periods, the number of poor will change. It is possible that some become poor and others escape poverty. Let's call the actual and counterfactual number of poor in periods 0 and 1, respectively, q_0 and q_1^*. We can then define the change in poverty between periods 1 and 0 as

$$(8) \qquad P_1^* - P_0 = \frac{1}{n} \sum_{i=1}^{q_1^*} \frac{z - y_{i1}}{z} - \frac{1}{n} \sum_{i=1}^{q_0} \frac{z - y_{i0}}{z}.$$

Let's now order the individuals, so that the poor in both periods are from $i = 1, \dots q_{11}^*$, those moving into poverty $i = q_{11}^* + 1, \dots q_{01}^*$ (that is, nonpoor in period 0 and poor in period 1), those moving out of poverty $i = q_{01}^* + 1$, $\dots q_{10}^*$, and finally, those nonpoor in each period $i = q_{10}^* + 1, \dots n$. Then equation 8 can be written as

$$(9) \quad P_1^* - P_0 = \frac{1}{n} \sum_{i=1}^{q_{11}^*} \left(\frac{z - y_{i1}^*}{z} - \frac{z - y_{i0}}{z} \right) + \frac{1}{n} \sum_{i=q_{11}^*+1}^{q_{01}^*} \frac{z - y_{i1}^*}{z} - \frac{1}{n} \sum_{i=q_{01}^*+1}^{q_{10}^*} \frac{z - y_{i0}}{z}$$

that is, the changes in the gap consist of the change of the gap of those poor in both periods, plus the gap of those poor in the second but not in the first period, minus the gap in the first period of those leaving poverty.[7] Dividing the left and right sides of equation 9 by $(P_1^* - P_0)$ yields a decomposition in terms of the contribution to the total poverty change of those staying poor, those becoming poor, and those leaving poverty. Note that this is an exact decomposition.

Equation 9 can be rewritten in terms of changes in real income. The part in parentheses in the first term of equation 9 is directly defined in terms of $y_{i1}^* - y_{i0} = X_i$. We can also premultiply the terms with the summation sign for each of the two subsequent terms by $(y_{i0} - y_{i1}^*)/ (y_{i0} - y_{i1}^*)$. Slightly rewritten, equation 9 becomes

$$(10)\ P_1^* - P_0 = \frac{1}{n} \sum_{i=1}^{q_{11}^*} \left(\frac{y_{i0} - y_{i1}^*}{z} \right) + \frac{1}{n} \sum_{i=q_{11}^*+1}^{q_{01}^*} \frac{y_{i0} - y_{i1}^*}{z} \frac{z - y_{i1}^*}{y_{i0} - y_{i1}^*} - \frac{1}{n} \sum_{i=q_{01}^*+1}^{q_{10}^*} \frac{z - y_{i0}}{y_{i0} - y_{i1}^*} \frac{y_{i0} - y_{i1}^*}{z}$$

or

$$(11) \quad P_1^* - P_0 = \frac{1}{n} \sum_{i=1}^{q_{11}^*} \left(\frac{-X_i}{z} \right) + \frac{1}{n} \sum_{i=q_{11}^*+1}^{q_{01}^*} \left(\frac{-X_i}{z} \right) \frac{z - y_{i1}^*}{y_{i0} - y_{i1}^*} - \frac{1}{n} \sum_{i=q_{01}^*+1}^{q_{10}^*} \frac{z - y_{i0}}{y_{i0} - y_{i1}^*} \left(\frac{-X_i}{z} \right).$$

This expression clearly suggests that when calculating the total counterfactual poverty change, for households that leave or enter into poverty, only the real income change up to or counting from the poverty line will be taken into account; for those that remain poor, their entire real income change is relevant. This allows us to define the share of the real income change that has to be taken into account as

(12a)
$$s_i^* = 1 \quad \text{for } q_i \in \left\{1, \ldots q_{11}^*\right\}$$

(12b)
$$s_i^* = \frac{z - y_{i1}^*}{y_{i0} - y_{i1}^*} \quad \text{for } q_i \in \left\{q_{11}^* + 1, \ldots q_{01}^*\right\} \text{ and}$$

(12c)
$$s_i^* = \frac{z - y_{i0}}{y_{i1}^* - y_{i0}} \quad \text{for } q_i \in \left\{q_{01}^* + 1, \ldots q_{10}^*\right\}.$$

Note that these shares s_i^* are dependent on the specific counterfactual studied (that is, they are endogenous). Furthermore, they are all between 0 and 1.

Using equations 12a, 12b, and 12c, equation 11 can be rewritten as

(13)
$$P_1^* - P_0 = \frac{1}{n} \sum_{i=1}^{q_{10}^*} s_i^* \left(\frac{-X_i}{z}\right).$$

Equation 13 is of only limited interest; if only one factor is considered in the counterfactual, the equation describes only what in practice is calculated via simulations. Calculating the weights s_i^* is probably more time-consuming than calculating the change in poverty directly from the derived and the actual distribution. Furthermore, equation 13 is restricted to very specific poverty measures, while microsimulations can handle any measure. Nevertheless, equation 13 becomes more interesting when X is itself determined by different variables.

SIMULATING AND DECOMPOSING THE IMPACT OF A GROUP OF VARIABLES

Consider a counterfactual that consists of two parts (V and W), and assume that for each i, $X_i = V_i + W_i$. Now equation 13 can be used to study the contribution of each factor V_i and W_i in the total counterfactual change. For a given total change in real income (that is, *for a given total counterfactual*), the shares $s_i{}^*$ will be constant, so that equation 13 can be written as

(14)
$$P_1^* - P_0 = \frac{1}{n}\sum_{i=1}^{q_{10}^*} s_i^*\left(\frac{-V_i}{z}\right) + \frac{1}{n}\sum_{i=1}^{q_{10}^*} s_i^*\left(\frac{-W_i}{z}\right).$$

This implies that for a given total change, the contribution of different factors to the change in poverty can be written as derived from equation 14. In particular, the contribution of factor V_i given total change X_i, $\theta(V|X)$ can be defined as

(15)
$$\theta\left(V_i\big|X_i\right) = \frac{\dfrac{1}{n}\displaystyle\sum_{i=1}^{q_{10}^*} s_i^*\left(\dfrac{-V_i}{z}\right)}{P_1^* - P_0}.$$

Note that these contributions sum to one, but also that they are always defined relative to a particular total counterfactual change. For example, let us define $P_1^V (P_1^W)$ as poverty in period 1 when $V (W)$ has been added to y_{i0}. Even though $(y_{i0} + X_i) = (y_{i0} + V_i + W_i)$, it can be easily seen that

(16)
$$P_1^* - P_0 \neq \left(P_1^V - P_0\right) + \left(P_1^W - P_0\right).$$

In other words, the total poverty change due to adding both V and W to real income is not simply equal to the poverty change induced by adding V and W separately. Obviously, this means that the decomposition has to be carefully interpreted. Equations 14 and 15 will be used below to interpret the contribution to poverty changes of different elements linked to economic reform.

LINKING POVERTY AND GROWTH: AN OVERALL ASSESSMENT

The decomposition described above provides a simple way of assessing the contribution of different factors to a particular counterfactual poverty change. One counterfactual is of particular interest for the current research: assessing the contribution of different factors to the *actual observed* total change in poverty $(P_1 - P_0)$. With an appropriate residual term (ε_i), equation 5 provides a prediction model for changes in real income for each person, based on different factors. In other words, suppose $X_i = V_i + W_i + \varepsilon_i$. Equation 13 can then be rewritten (we drop the asterisks, since the counterfactual considered is the actual change in poverty) as

$$(17) \quad P_1 - P_0 = \frac{1}{n}\sum_{i=1}^{q_{10}} s_i\left(\frac{-V_i}{z}\right) + \frac{1}{n}\sum_{i=1}^{q_{10}} s_i\left(\frac{-W_i}{z}\right) + \frac{1}{n}\sum_{i=1}^{q_{10}} s_i\left(\frac{-\varepsilon_i}{z}\right).$$

Equation 17 then provides simple ways of describing the contribution of these different factors (and the error term) to the observed poverty changes, using shares s_i, which are based on the *actual* observed poverty transitions.

Equation 17 shows a direct link between changes in individual incomes over time and the poverty outcome. Furthermore, replacing the income change by the predicted contribution of different factors using equation 5 and dividing each term by the total poverty change gives the contribution of these factors to the change in poverty. For example, let $\theta_{\Delta pi}$ be the contribution of changes in output prices to the total poverty change and $\theta_{\Delta ki}$ be the contribution to the total poverty change of changes in particular endowments k, then using equations 5 and 17, these contributions to the total poverty change are defined as

$$(18a) \quad \theta_{\Delta p_i} = \frac{-\dfrac{1}{n}\displaystyle\sum_{i=1}^{q_{10}} s_i \varphi_{t+1}^* \Delta \ln p_i}{z \cdot \left(P_1 - P_0\right)}$$

$$(18b) \quad \theta_{\Delta k_i} = \frac{-\dfrac{1}{n}\displaystyle\sum_{i=1}^{q_{10}} s_i \beta_{t+1}^* \Delta \ln k_i}{z \cdot \left(P_1 - P_0\right)}.$$

The overall result is a decomposition of the poverty gap into the effects of changes in fixed endowments, changes in input and output prices, and random events, *for a given total change in poverty*. The decomposition will now be applied to data related to 1989 and 1994–95, before and after a major set of reform measures were implemented. The decomposition of income changes in equation 5 is exact when using an estimation method that imposes that the sum of the residuals is zero, such as OLS. But the proposed decomposition is done on a subsample only, so this property does not hold. Consequently, decompositions based on equation 17 are not exact and the contribution of the error term will have to be added

$$(19) \qquad \theta_\varepsilon = \frac{-\dfrac{1}{n}\displaystyle\sum_{i=1}^{q_{10}} s_i \varepsilon_i}{z \cdot (P_1 - P_0)}.$$

NOTES

1. The discussion in part 2 builds on Dercon (2001).

2. Note the implication that to keep the analysis tractable and simple, recursivity is assumed between consumption and production. In general, this is not easily justified since it is clear that many markets are imperfect in Ethiopia, including land, credit, and insurance markets. The reasons include the standard theoretical ones, as well as some specific cases, such as in the case of land, extensive restrictions for political purposes, which will be discussed below. The nature of food market interventions may also have implied a breakdown of recursivity, as will be discussed further. In the econometric analysis, the fact that panel data are used allows heterogeneity across households to be addressed, including in (shadow) prices, so that the recursivity assumption is less restrictive than it may seem.

3. Note that this allows for changes over time in the marginal value product of particular fixed factors beyond changes brought about by shifts in the prices of output and variable inputs.

4. Datt and Ravallion (1992) developed a simple decomposition in growth and distribution effects of changes in poverty; however, this is not an exact decomposition, because the contribution of different factors cannot be directly derived from the decomposition.

5. By using ln Y, the result is effectively the same as when using the Watts measure. Since the poverty gap is more commonly used in discussions of changes in poverty, the problem is stated in terms of this index. In the econometric analysis, the results could have been presented on a linear (rather than log-linear) profit function defined in terms of Y rather than ln Y. While the theoretical foundations for such a profit function are weaker (one could think of it as a Leontief model but without most of the interaction terms), it provides a poverty change decomposition directly defined over the standard poverty gap

measure, which is defined in terms of the level of income. The Watts poverty measure is defined over the log of Y, so it is a natural candidate to use in the decomposition.

6. In this exposition, I do not consider attrition in the panel. As discussed below in the data set used, attrition rates were very low in the period considered.

7. As suggested earlier and using the notation as before, the Watts poverty measure is defined as

$$W_t = \frac{1}{n} \sum_{i=1}^{q_t} z - y_{it}$$

so that the decomposition in (8) is, in practice, a decomposition of the Watts poverty measure. Just as the squared poverty gap, it is convex in levels of real income, implying that income levels far below the poverty line have a higher weight than levels closer to the poverty line—unlike the poverty gap, which is linear in levels of income.

CHAPTER 6

Econometric Model and Results

I n this chapter, we investigate the determinants of the changes in food consumption during the study period, 1989 to 1994–95. First, we discuss the specification used to estimate the generic model described in equation 5 in chapter 5. The goal is to establish whether the economic reforms (through their impact on prices and incomes) are responsible for the observed changes, rather than other factors, such as demographic change, illness shocks, or climatic variability. We will estimate a number of different specifications, in order to establish the robustness of the results. Furthermore, we present decompositions that quantify the contribution of the different factors that determine the changes in real food consumption based on the regression estimates. The estimates will then be used in chapter 7 to conduct a decomposition of poverty changes. Introducing an error term, e_{t+1}, equation 5 from chapter 5 can be rewritten as an econometric model that explains changes in real income over time in terms of any shift in output prices, input prices, fixed input changes, and shocks (such as rainfall or idiosyncratic events). Since the technology used during this period, 1989–95, probably changed because of the reorganization of the activity portfolio, changes in the coefficients are also allowed for. A general change in total factor productivity (that is, technological progress) is measured by a change in the constant in the underlying production function. The result is equation 20.

$$\Delta \ln Y_i = \eta + \varphi^*_{t+1} \Delta \ln p_i + \Delta \varphi^* \ln p_{it} + \sum_n \alpha^*_{nt+1} \Delta \ln p^x_{in} + \sum_n \Delta \alpha^*_n \ln p^x_{int}$$

(20)

$$+ \sum_j \beta^*_{jt+1} \Delta \ln k_{ij} + \sum_j \Delta \beta^*_j \ln k_{ijt} + \sum_m \gamma^*_{mt+1} \Delta \gamma^*_m \ln u_{imt} + e_{t+1}.$$

Since this is not a standard difference model, a few comments on the econometric implications of equation 20 are useful. By estimating this difference model by OLS, one effectively controls for fixed (level) effects—that is, household heterogeneity in the profit function, despite the fact that equation 20 includes terms in levels of prices and inputs. Household heterogeneity is typically an important issue in estimating profit or production functions, because many relevant variables that explain a household's outcomes typically remain unmeasured and may be correlated with some of the observed variables. For example, a farmer's ability to farm is important but may remain unobserved, or possibly correlated with other observed variables, which would bias the estimates on some variables included in the regression. Developing this example further, if the farmer's ability happens to be negatively correlated with land, so that small farmers are the best farmers, then the returns to land estimated in the regression excluding ability will be lower than the "true" value, implying a negative bias. If the source of heterogeneity that is missing in the regression is a fixed effect, a difference model will produce unbiased estimates on those variables that change over time. However, it can be shown that the coefficients on variables that do not change over time (but are included in the model to capture changes in coefficients) do not benefit from this property; in other words, they may still be biased. In fact, the estimated coefficients in equation 20 will be exactly the same as the difference of the coefficients if they would have been estimated using the level in equation 4 and using OLS for each year independently. Nevertheless, estimating these coefficients in equation 20 will be more efficient (Glewwe and Hall 1994).

Using equation 20 on the data requires careful justifications for the inclusion of the right-side variables. First, land and labor supply available to the household will be considered as fixed inputs, meaning that labor and land markets are assumed missing. Land is not tradable in Ethiopia; land is state-owned and allocated to peasants by a local council, and the peasants cannot buy or sell it. Land rental was illegal until the 1990s, but even after that point, cultivated land and owned land remain closely correlated.[1] Wage labor, for agriculture or other industry, remains relatively rare. Rural wage labor markets remain underdeveloped, although they are progressing relative to the period before 1989 when wage labor was forbidden. Nonetheless, informal labor transactions take place in the village, in the form of labor-sharing arrangements ("debbo" or "wenfel"). These arrangements are largely reciprocal, so the total labor available within the household remains the basis of these transactions. This means that these informal arrangements will not improve efficiency substantially; they will not substitute for the trade of labor between households with different labor endowments. Labor remains the basis of these transactions.

Consequently, and for simplicity, both the production factors, labor and land, are therefore considered fixed. The labor variable used in the empirical analysis includes male and female adults and children.[2] Landholdings are not homogeneous across the sample. There are substantial differences in soil fertility and agricultural potential within and across communities. Information from the survey is used to control for these differences. Changes in land and labor availability allow us to estimate the coefficients in equation 20, which are directly linked to marginal returns. It is assumed that soil fertility and potential have not changed in this period, 1989–95; while they may well have been changing over longer periods of time, the change in a five-year period is unlikely to be very important. At any rate, no information is available to control for this soil fertility.

Other fixed inputs include location and infrastructure, proxied by the presence and quality of roads and distances to urban centers. In community surveys, any changes in road presence and quality were investigated; however, these communities reported few changes. Consequently, these variables are only included to investigate changes in the returns to the fixed inputs location and infrastructure during this period, and not to calculate marginal returns to roads and distance from towns.

The most direct result of the reform program appears to have been the changes in agricultural output prices; in five out of the six communities considered, the terms of trade improved. (This price change will be included in the analysis.) Crop-related income is, however, not the only source of income; the estimated value of the harvest contributed only about 43 percent to total income in 1994. Even though this is likely to have been a conservative estimate of the true relevance of crop income, noncrop income, such as business income or livestock product sales, is also important. Unfortunately, price information is not available on these noncrop sources; however, this is not a serious shortcoming in the current context. On the one hand, most of these activities involve substantial inputs from local crop agriculture, such as the raw materials for much of the small-scale food trade or food processing. The terms of trade for these noncrop products are then likely to increase to a similar extent as the producer terms of trade for different crops. The producer terms of trade changes would then capture the increased returns quite well. On the other hand, since these noncrop activities typically involve some trading with urban areas, the shadow price for noncrop activities may well be proxied by the inclusion of infrastructure and distance variables in the empirical specification of equation 20. Although very few purchased inputs tend to be used in both farm and off-farm activities, they should also be included. Again, no data are available on this. Nevertheless, since they tend to be supplied via nearby urban centers, the relative movement of these input prices may well be captured through the inclusion of the infrastructure and distance variables.

The arguments in the preceding paragraphs lead us to a reduced-form specification in which agricultural output prices, infrastructure, and distance variables allow for the identification of a direct effect of the reform policies on real incomes through price changes. Changes in labor and land allow us to identify the marginal (physical) products underlying the production process. The levels of these fixed inputs at $t + 1$ provide us with evidence on any *changes* in the marginal products that affect the marginal return to inputs beyond price changes (see equations 3 and 4 in chapter 5). This may seem problematic, since it suggests that the underlying production technology has changed. Nevertheless, a reform program, by changing the overall incentive structure for both agricultural and non-agricultural activities, may well have affected the relative (physical) returns to land, labor, and infrastructure. This could have been achieved through a more efficient use of resources, in response to the restrictions being lifted on crop choice (via the quota system) or increasing mobility beyond those measured by price changes.[3] Furthermore, given that the left-side variable is effectively a composite commodity consisting of farm and nonfarm activities, shifts in the production function may be a reflection of a relative shift of the composition of the activities. For example, if reforms restore the returns to agriculture, then crop-related activities may become relatively more important in the portfolio of activities in terms of the allocation of time and other inputs. This would result in a higher contribution of land to profits, which would be linked to an increase in its marginal product.

Observed changes in real income are likely to have been affected by both common and idiosyncratic shocks as well. Ideally, detailed information on these shocks should have been used, but considerable detail was missing from the 1989 survey. Nevertheless, two key variables are available: rainfall, both long-term changes and changes in the last year, and episodes of serious adult illness in the period between the two survey rounds.[4] The latter is likely to be the most important type of idiosyncratic shock.[5] Controlling for such shocks is crucial for a correct interpretation of the effects of policy, because marginal returns to land and labor are bound to be sensitive to shocks.

The result of our discussion in this chapter is an econometric model that explains changes in the log of real income (that is, the growth between t and $t + 1$) in terms of changes in fixed endowments and changes in their returns, changing real prices, and common and idiosyncratic shocks. Let's define p_{it}^a as agricultural output prices; T_{it} as labor available in year t; L_{it} as land available in year t; I^k_{it} as a vector of K location and/or infrastructure characteristics in year t; $\Delta \ln S_i$ as the illness shock; and $\Delta \ln R_i$ as the change in rainfall in $t + 1$ relative to t. The econometric model can then be defined as

$$
(21) \quad \begin{aligned}
\Delta \ln Y_i &= \eta + \beta^1_{t+1}\Delta \ln T_i + \Delta \beta^1_t \ln T_{it} + \beta^2_{t+1}\Delta \ln L_i + \Delta \beta^2_t \ln L_{it} \\
&+ \sum_k \Delta \alpha_k \ln I^k_{it} + \varphi^*_{t+1}\Delta \ln p_i^a + \gamma^1_{t+1}\Delta \ln S_i + \gamma^2_{t+1}\Delta \ln R_i + e_{it+1}.
\end{aligned}
$$

Another issue is how to create an appropriate proxy for real income (the left-side variable). As previously mentioned, income was not very well measured in the survey, especially when comparing incomes over time. Consumption, at least food consumption, was much more carefully and consistently measured. This inconsistency presents both problems and opportunities. First, consumption is hardly the same as income as a concept when measuring returns; however, since it is likely to be less sensitive to current circumstances, it will be a better reflection of the household's perceived typical return to its own assets and endowments. By the same token, to the extent that all the shocks and events affecting the household are not well measured, consumption provides a way to assess the impact of reforms on living standards. It is important to note that food consumption is typically a very high share of total consumption (in 1994 it was close to 80 percent). Furthermore, since the income elasticity of nonfood items is likely to be higher than that for basic food items, using food consumption underestimates the true response to reforms (although admittedly also to shocks, such as rainfall). Therefore, using food consumption is unlikely to fundamentally affect linking data on the reforms to outcomes. If anything, it biases the results against any impact of the reforms, in favor of an interpretation linked to shocks. By using consumption in equation 21, the link with a welfare interpretation becomes more straightforward. Furthermore, a decomposition of poverty defined more appropriately in terms of consumption, rather than income, can be then performed.

Table 18 gives the estimation results, and table 19 gives the decomposition. Six different specifications are considered.[6] Each model is a difference model, which allows for fixed effects. Mean values are given in the last column. The left-side variable is the change in the log of real consumption, which can be viewed as the five-year growth rate. Consequently, the regression gives the contribution of different variables to the consumption growth. Recall that this is an econometric model based on equation 20, including as right-side variables both variables defined as differences between 1989 and 1994–95, and variables defined in terms of levels in 1994–95. As evident from equation 20, the estimated coefficients on right-hand variables defined in terms of differences will give the coefficients explaining real income in 1994–95, while estimated coefficients on level variables in 1989 will give the increase in these coefficients since 1989 (see also equations 4 and 5). Growth between 1989 and 1994 is

Table 18. Econometric Model Real Income Function: Dependent Variable Was Change in Log Consumption between 1989 and 1994

Item	Model 1 coeff	p value	Model 2 coeff	p value	Model 3 coeff	p value	Model 4 coeff	p value	Model 5 coeff	p value	Model 6 coeff	p value	Sample mean
Constant	0.23	0.37	0.26	0.27	-0.11	0.68	0.00	0.99	0.18	0.15			1.000
ln(land in 89 ha + 0.1)	0.21	0.13	0.21	0.17	0.21	0.17							0.294
ln(soil quality)	0.20	0.21	0.20	0.21	0.23	0.20							-0.041
ln(augmented land)							0.21	0.13	0.20	0.11	0.19	0.11	0.160
Δ ln(land in ha + 0.1)	0.24	0.04	0.24	0.05	0.23	0.05	0.24	0.03	0.22	0.03	0.22	0.02	0.327
ln(adults in 89)	-0.08		-0.08	0.19	-0.08	0.24	-0.08	0.30	-0.06	0.46			1.549
Δ ln(adult equiv.)	0.30	0.31	0.30	0.31	0.31	0.28	0.31	0.26	0.32	0.23	0.35	0.21	0.091
ln(male ad. in 89 + 1)	-0.02	0.96											0.797
ln(fem ad. in 89 + 1)	-0.07	0.78											0.864
ln(children in 89 + 1)	-0.04	0.81											1.379
Δ ln(male ad. + 1)	0.25	0.26											0.176
Δ ln(fem. ad. + 1)	0.02	0.89											0.133
Δ ln(children + 1)	0.14	0.55											-0.087
ln(yrs ad. educ. + 1)	0.01	0.97	0.01	0.96	0.03	0.88	0.03	0.88	0.01	0.96	0.01	0.96	0.202
ln(ad. serious ill. + 1)	-0.22	0.36	-0.22	0.37	-0.22	0.37	-0.22	0.38	-0.20	0.39	-0.19	0.43	0.188
Dummy Dinki	-0.14	0.26	-0.17	0.14	0.04	0.78	0.55	0.07					0.150
Dummy D. Berhan	0.16	0.16	0.13	0.12	0.37	0.05	0.03	0.80					0.175
Dummy Adele Keke	0.44	0.02	0.42	0.03	0.71	0.02	0.30	0.09					0.121

	(1)	(2)	(3)	(4)	(5)	(6)
Dummy Gara Godo	−0.02 (0.92)	−0.06 (0.78)	0.48 (0.20)	0.52 (0.01)		0.155
Dummy Domaa	0.58 (0.00)	0.57 (0.00)	0.72 (0.00)	0.24 (0.38)		0.144
Δ (% real prod. prices)	0.55 (0.07)	0.60 (0.00)		0.37 (0.12)	0.59 (0.00)	0.263
Δ ln(rain last 5 years)				1.15 (0.06)		0.002
Δ ln(rain last season)				0.22 (0.45)		−0.179
Δ ln(rain 5 yrs*seas.)				0.43 (0.04)		−0.177
ln(distance to town)				−0.24 (0.21)	−0.28 (0.08)	0.000
Road infrastructure?				0.17 (0.40)	0.27 (0.03)	0.706
F joint	$F(16,377 = 2.73)$	$F(13,341 = 3.63)$	$F(13,340 = 3.54)$	$F(12,341 = 3.85)$	$F(11,342 = 4.15)$	$F(9,345) = 10.59$
Adjusted R^2	0.072	0.082	0.085	0.088	0.089	

Testing restrictions labor levels equal? $F(2,337) = 0.01$

Lab. changes equal? $F(2,337) = 0.74$

Land terms equal? $F(2,340) = 0.01$

Land terms equal? 0.088

Constant, lnaeu89 $F(2,344) = 1.03$

Rain variables equal? $F(1,344) = 1.30$

Note: Mean 0.3733, $n = 354$; robust standard errors corrected for village cluster effects.

Table 19. Decomposition of Real Consumption Growth
(percent)

Item	Model					
	1	2	3	4	5	6
Increase in land	0.21	0.21	0.21	0.20	0.20	0.19
Increase in adult labor	0.09	0.07	0.08	0.07	0.08	0.09
Change in returns to land (tech. shift)	0.14	0.14	0.14	0.09	0.08	0.08
Change in returns to labor (tech. shift)	−0.32	−0.34	−0.31	−0.31	−0.24	
Changes in returns to education of adults	0.01	0.01	0.02	0.02	0.01	0.01
Crop producer prices change			0.39	0.41	0.26	0.42
Change returns to infrastructure/location					0.32	0.51
Relative rainfall shock					−0.10	−0.20
Effect of illness shocks	−0.11	−0.11	−0.11	−0.11	−0.10	−0.10
Village-level effect	0.98	1.02	0.59	0.62		
Constant effect					0.49	
Sum of all effects	1.00	1.00	1.00	1.00	1.00	1.00

Note: Total change = 37 percent.

therefore shown to come from increases in endowments and prices, and increases in the returns relative to 1989, controlling for shocks.

The first specification uses fixed village-level effects; that is, all village-level variables (for example, prices) are perfectly captured by a set of dummies. The model includes landholdings and an index of land quality. It is a subjective index, scaled relative to the village-level mean.[7] Three types of available labor are considered: male and female adults (above age 15) and children above the age of 5. The model also lists the average years of education for adults. Note that, on average, educational levels are extremely low, below one year per adult. These levels are assumed to have remained constant between 1989 and 1994, so only the change in the returns is measured.[8] The model also includes an idiosyncratic shock: the average number of serious adult illness episodes between 1989 and 1994 per adult in the family.[9] The results show significant effects on changes in landholdings and levels of land in 1989, and on some of the fixed village-level effects.

The econometric results show significant effects on the variables measuring changes in landholdings and levels of land in 1989, and on some of the fixed village-level effects included in the model. The land variables imply that growth is partly explained by some increases in total landholdings in some villages (21 percent of total growth; see table 19), but also by an increase in the marginal (physical) return to land since 1989, with an additional effect for those with higher soil quality. This can be understood as a shift in the income portfolio toward more land-intensive activities (that is, agriculture) in line with the incentives provided by the reform process; household income is now produced by a more land-intensive technology, with a higher growth effect for households with better land. The education effect is low and not significant; recall that educational levels are extremely low in this sample, so that the total contribution to growth is very small.[10] The largest effect comes from village fixed effects, suggesting that relative prices and changes in the returns to local conditions dominate overall growth (98 percent). Illness shocks are negative, and even though they are insignificant, they reduced average growth by 11 percent.

Household labor composition does not appear to matter significantly in this specification. It appears, however, that the different labor variables could be taken together: a test of a linear restriction stating equality of coefficients on the level and changes in labor could not be rejected ($F(4,337) = 0.19$). Alternative specifications with total household size or adult-equivalent units (as used in the previous sections) gave very similar results, so from column 2 the labor variables are restricted to one measure in terms of adult-equivalent units.[11] As expected, the results show a positive effect on changes in labor, which explains 7 percent of total growth. Although insignificant, it appears that the technology used in 1994 is less labor intensive, which reduces the marginal returns of labor and contributes a negative 34 percent to growth. This is consistent with the shift toward more land-intensive activities. Note that if the reforms aimed to stimulate more labor-intensive rural production, then this was not achieved. Also, if the poor have typically more labor than other assets, this would have contributed to a relatively low poverty elasticity of the growth process in this period.

In the next four columns, price and community level information are added. In model 3, the percentage change of crop producer prices is added (see table 11, chapter 4 for details). It was constructed to reflect changes in household price incentives, so that the community fixed effects can remain. Given the presence of the fixed effects, its significance (at 7 percent) is encouraging. Its coefficient directly measures price responsiveness; that is, the output elasticity is the coefficient minus one. However, the value of 0.55 has to be interpreted with caution. Since household real income is more than just crops, it could be compared with the share of crop income in total income. In 1994 this share was 43 percent, suggesting that an aggregate crop output elasticity of about 28 percent (0.55/0.43 minus one). Nevertheless, since it was shown before that many other activities are closely related to crops, and their prices may have similarly shifted, this must be seen as an upper bound. In any case, the average producer price increase clearly linked to the reforms explains the approximate 39 percent of total growth.

Since the different land variables appear to be having very similar effects, column 4 introduces a further restriction by using "augmented" land as a variable—that is, the product of the land and the soil variable, further multiplied by a control variable for "agricultural potential." Since land and soil (on the basis of the available information) cannot easily be compared across areas in terms of potential (both physical and monetary), a variable measuring this was added to model 4.[12] A linear restriction on the three land variables was then found not to be rejected ($F(2,340)$ = 0.01), so augmented land was used subsequently. Note that all variables have similar effects in the decomposition as in models 1 to 3.

In columns 5 and 6, the community fixed effects are replaced by rainfall, infrastructure, and location variables. The inclusion of these variables in the regression did not change the effects and contribution of the household-level variables, which suggests that they may proxy the main community-level influences reasonably well. The argument to support this view is that since the village-level fixed effects capture perfectly the community-level prices and conditions, any substantive change in the other coefficients would suggest missing community-level variables. Nevertheless, the results will have to be interpreted with caution since there is evidence of multicollinearity between community characteristics and only limited scope for introducing other information in the regression (given only six different communities). The particular variables were chosen to explain the regression provided that they did not change the effects and contribution of the household-level variables. In particular, since fixed effects capture perfectly the community-level prices and conditions, any substantive change in the other coefficients would suggest missing community-level variables. Nevertheless, the results will have to be interpreted with caution since there is evidence of multicollinearity between community characteristics and only limited scope for introducing information in the regression (given only six different communities).

Since real consumption is used on the left-hand side, measured outcomes reflect household strategies to cope with the consequences of risk, such as credit and savings. Any effect on rainfall variables, especially short-term rainfall, therefore reflects uninsured risk. Also, introducing the long-term rainfall experience would be relevant; one year of poor rains may well be handled within the household through asset transactions, but several years of poor rainfall would be much harder to accommodate. Still, if households have a difficult time handling shocks, then more recent rainfall should matter for outcomes. Without further analysis on smoothing behavior, it seems appropriate to consider the effects of both the short- and long-term rainfall. Consequently, relative rainfall is used in the most recent crop season (comparing 1994–95 with 1989), and the relative average rainfall in the five years preceding each survey round. In column 5, both measurements are positive, but only long-term rainfall appears significant. However, since the variables are highly correlated, introducing either gave significant outcomes of at least 6 percent, while a linear restriction imposing equality of both effects could not be rejected ($F(1,344) = 1.30$). In column 6, this equality was imposed.

For road infrastructure, the variable reported is whether the village has a road (either an all-weather road or a dirt road). Other finer distinctions were not significant. A measure of relative remoteness was constructed using the distance to the nearest town, scaled by the mean distance to the nearest town in the sample. In column 5, these were both insignificant, but once further restrictions were tested and imposed (including on rainfall, but also dropping the constant and the number of adults in 1989, the latter both individually and jointly insignificant), they became strongly significant.

Good rainfall typically boosts growth. In 1993–94, rains were (as discussed previously) on average not as good as in 1988–89 (contrary to the national experience), even though slightly better in the period 1990–94 compared to the period 1985–89. The overall result suggests that rainfall kept growth down by about a fifth. The effect on roads means that returns to infrastructure have strongly increased since 1989. Again, this suggests that reforms, which encourage more trade-oriented activities, have contributed to growth, despite higher transport or traded input costs. Nevertheless, even though the war did not directly affect the villages concerned, it allowed for increased mobility of goods and people with increased security. Similarly, the effect on distance suggests that proximity to towns contributed positively to growth, and remoteness contributed negatively to growth. The total contribution to growth of infrastructure and location is about 51 percent, which underlies its importance in this period.

In conclusion, according to our econometric decomposition, better returns to roads and, to a lesser extent, remoteness contributed the most to growth between 1989 and 1994–95. As a consequence, the model predicts that those with poor location and no infrastructure would have had only half the growth rate of the others during this period of reform and return to peace. Better crop prices also contributed a very high share, 42 percent. Acquiring more fixed assets is obviously positive; the increases in landholding (this was particularly true in one village, Korodegaga, following the disbanding of the producer cooperative) and more labor add to real household income. However, their overall contribution in this period remains relatively small. Returns to education also appear to have increased considerably, but low average levels of education mean that only a small increase has occurred in this period. An interesting finding is that an increase in returns to land through its marginal product suggests a shift to a more land-intensive production mode. On average, the effect contributes only 8 percent to growth, but it means that those with more land will have seen higher growth rates. Furthermore, since this effect also includes an additional return to better soil quality and higher potential, effects across the distribution may be larger; those in low potential areas or with relatively poor soil would have had a lower growth rate from the same levels of land. In other words, any shift toward a more agriculturally based production mode will have given disproportionate growth to farmers with more land. Finally, poor rains and illness kept growth down by about a third.

How robust are these results? As previously mentioned, the design of the questionnaire resulted in problems with income measurement for comparative purposes. Nevertheless, in table 20, the regressions of model 6 are performed using total real income (with decompositions in table 21). The first column uses the log of real total gross income changes, while column two reports the results excluding livestock sales income (this exclusion is because gross income including livestock sales may include substantial asset transactions that probably should not be counted as income). Illness shocks were dropped since they refer to a much longer period, while the number of adults in 1989 was added again, since the regressions confirmed the earlier discussion of a possible shift away from labor to a land-intensive mode of production, even though the coefficient is again not significant. Using real consumption, the effects are remarkably consistent with those reported, with roads and crop prices dominating the effects.

Table 20. Robustness Test: Using Real Income with and without Livestock Sales Income

Item	Total income		Income without livestock sales	
	Coefficient	p value	Coefficient	p value
ln(augmented land)	0.21	0.16	0.15	0.27
Δ ln(land in ha + 0.1)	0.47	0.01	0.36	0.02
Δ ln(adult equiv.)	0.34	0.07	0.34	0.05
ln(adults in 89)	0.03	0.92	−0.13	0.61
ln(yrs adult educ. + 1)	0.18	0.53	0.36	0.36
Δ (% real prod. prices)	0.83	0.01	0.92	0.01
Δ ln(rain 5 yrs*seas.)	0.12	0.52	0.48	0.10
ln(distance to town)	0.19	0.50	−0.08	0.78
Road infrastructure	0.15	0.78	0.44	0.41
Joint sign. $F_{(9,322)}$	16.77		14.25	

Note: $n = 342$. Same specification as in model 6, except for serious illness and ln(adults in 1989), robust standard errors corrected for clustering.

Table 21. Decomposition of Income Regression (Table 20) as a Percentage of Total Contribution

Item	Total income	Income without livestock
Increase in land	0.26	0.23
Increases in adult labor	0.05	0.06
Change in returns to land (tech. shift)	0.06	0.05
Change in returns to labor (tech. shift)	0.07	−0.40
Changes in returns to education of adults	0.06	0.14
Crop producer prices change	0.36	0.47
Change returns to infrastructure/location	0.18	0.61
Relative rainfall shock	−0.04	−0.17
Total	1.00	1.00
Mean change	0.60	0.51

The core findings largely depend on the ability to disentangle the price change effects from the effects of shocks, such as rainfall. Note first that most effects, including the effect on prices, remain stable after introducing the community-level variables. This supports the view that the price changes are genuine; that is, they are not caused by temporary (village-level) price movements, such as are caused by bad rains. Nevertheless, OLS—by attempting to perfectly predict mean real income changes— may affect the findings as well. To check the robustness of the specification further, two alternative approaches were used. First, it could be argued that poor households have a different ability to respond to real price changes, even given differences in land, labor, and location (which the regression controls for). To test this, interaction terms were used on the key variables to check whether there was any sign of different behavior for the poor in 1989 versus the nonpoor. Both the effects on rainfall and on real prices were insignificant (at 52 and 17 percent, respectively). Second, quantile regressions were used to re-estimate model 6 (at the 33th, 50th, and 66th percentiles). The results were largely unchanged: strongly significant price results; price and infrastructure/location effects of similar size, in terms of the decomposition; and a strong negative effect of rainfall.[13]

There may be other concerns related to the specification. The choice of land and labor as fixed factors was discussed before. It is possible to treat these fixed factors as endogenous to the model by estimating shadow prices for them and then including these estimated prices in the regression model. For this we need identifying instruments, and the likely candidates for identification would be assets and demographic variables, such as land owned and available labor. The specification we have used can then be viewed as a reduced form specification of an approach without fixed factors; that way the results are unlikely to be much different. Second, it could be argued that other variables should be included in the survey. A variety of variables were introduced; for example, age of the head of household, and its square (as a proxy for farming experience), was not significant. Also, readers familiar with Ethiopia may wonder why oxen or livestock were not included as a determinant in the growth regression. Oxen are very important in most farming systems, but they can hardly be seen as a fixed asset, since they can be freely acquired in the market. They would be endogenous to the model, not least because oxen and other cattle are the most important form of savings, which is the alternative to spending income on consumption goods; these animals are actively accumulated. Furthermore, livestock and oxen ownership is positively correlated with land (whether augmented or not). Introducing livestock (unit value) prices gave insignificant results, but this may be linked to multicollinearity with rainfall, which is positively correlated. Lower prices for livestock contribute 7 percent to growth in this expanded version of model 6. The dramatic change in real consumption for some households raises the suspicion that a lot of the movement in real consumption is just measurement error. A starting point for investigating this potential error is simply to run an autoregressive model; that is, to regress changes on the lagged value of real consumption. The lower (closer to –1) the estimated coefficient on the value of consumption in 1989, the more the movement presents just "noise." In our case, the value was –0.81, significantly different from one, but still quite high. However, once we include the variables used in model 6, this value drops to –0.21; that is, a much higher persistence in consumption once the explanatory variables are accounted for. There is little reason to suspect measurement error in consumption to be specifically correlated with values included in the regression (for example, why would those with roads or those after 1989 that had high crop price increases systematically have underreported consumption in 1989 or overreported in 1994?). Consequently, measurement error is unlikely to undermine our conclusions.

NOTES

1. Before 1989, any form of land rental was also illegal, with some exceptions related to widows, disabled people, or families of serving soldiers. Sharecropping is relatively widespread and the simple set-up of the regressions does really account for this, except that it is considered as one part of the portfolio of activities to allocate land and labor, given relative endowments and prices faced. Although the number of sharecropping transactions are relatively high—in the cereal farming system, up to 20 percent of villages are engaged in it—the land areas involved remain relatively small. For example, the correlation between household landholdings suitable for cultivation and actual land size cultivated per household (after transactions) is above 90 percent.

2. Children are considered from the age of five upwards. In the survey, it was found that children performed a variety of farm- and nonfarm-related activities. Gross primary school enrollment rates in 1994 were only about 20 percent.

3. Any changes in the returns to roads and distances may also be linked to the effects of the return to peace.

4. The question asked in 1994 regarding illness queried whether any household member had suffered a serious, life-threatening illness in the last five years. Length of illness was also queried.

5. Dercon and Krishnan (2000) report that shocks to labor supply, such as illness and death of household head, have very important effects on welfare in rural Ethiopia. About 40 percent of households in the Ethiopian Rural Household Survey mentioned it as a cause of serious hardship in the last 20 years, after harvest failure; drought (78 percent) and the policy measures of the Derg (42 percent) were mentioned the most often.

6. All variables, except for dummies, are expressed in logs. Since some variables have zero values in the sample, 1 was added to those variables involved. The exception is land, where only 0.1 was added. The reason is that the bias involved in adding arbitrary constants can be large, especially if the constant added is close to the mean value of the variable.

   As a simple means of investigating this in the current sample, regressions were repeated for samples without zero values for particular variables. In the case of land, if 1 was added, coefficients on land and on other variables were very different compared to a sample, excluding landless households in 1989. If 0.1 was added, virtually identical coefficients were returned.

7. Households were asked to categorize their land according to three local well-known concepts of land quality ("lem," "lem-teuf," and "teuf"), equivalent to good, medium, and poor quality. The meaning of each of the three is unlikely to be comparable across widely varying farming systems, but within villages the comparisons are likely to be consistent.

8. Because of lack of data on education in 1989, the 1994 values are assumed to be valid for 1989. This is unlikely to be a problem, given the low enrollment rates in Ethiopia (by 1994, gross primary enrollment was only about 20 percent) and the collapse of the educational system by the end of the 1990s.

9. Serious illness shocks were defined as life-threatening illness episodes, affecting the individual for a considerable length of time. Recall was used in 1994 to collect information about all adults in this respect.

10. A few other educational variables were tried as well, such as literacy or whether any household member had an education. In none of the specifications used were these terms significant.

11. Strictly speaking, the F-test reported suggests a multiplicative labor term, not an additive term (such as household size). Results remained similar, while the interpretation is more straightforward when adding up adults.

12. It was constructed as a log of the village-level average yield per hectare times the village-level unit value per kilogram in 1989, scaled by the mean. The result in that mean potential (just as mean soil quality) in the sample is one for the mean household. Mean augmented landholdings are then equal to actual landholdings.

13. To allow comparison with the other results, the decomposition still used mean characteristics.

CHAPTER 7

Explaining Real Income Changes of the Poor

In the previous chapter, we explored the determinants of income changes in the period between 1989 and 1994–95 in the sample. We estimated an econometric model and presented a decomposition of the factors explaining the changes in real income. The method used gave an exact decomposition of the changes of the average household in the sample. In this chapter, we focus on the experiences of households across the income distribution, with an emphasis on the poor. We can distinguish four groups in the sample: some households were poor in both 1989 and 1994–95, others remained nonpoor in both periods, a number of households drifted into poverty between 1989 and 1994–95, and others escaped from poverty.

First, we will discuss some of the characteristics of these four groups. Then we will use the estimates of the econometric model obtained in the previous chapter to quantify the role played by the determinants of real income changes for each of the four groups. Table 22 lists many characteristics of the poor in 1989 and 1994–95. Income and livestock changes are consistent with consumption for each group of those poor in either period. The largest increases in landholdings were for those moving out of poverty. Patterns in mean landholdings are consistent with poverty in each round of the survey. Those poor in both periods have the least land. Cultivating chat is correlated with being nonpoor and moving out of poverty by 1994, while coffee is not (recall that the village that grew coffee suffered a bad coffee harvest in 1994). Fertilizer use does appear to be strongly related to poverty; those moving out of poverty and the nonpoor are more likely to use more fertilizer in 1994–95 than they did before. Livestock and business income increased most for the nonpoor, but the largest effect for those becoming nonpoor is from higher crop income. Those becoming poor in 1994 suffered declines in crop incomes. The persistently poor and those becoming poor witnessed the largest increases in labor supply within the household, in terms of adults or adult equivalents. Those becoming nonpoor have the most education, but the education levels still remain very low. Those remaining poor and those becoming poor live the farthest from towns, even though, in terms of the presence of a road connection, there is little difference between the various groups.

Nevertheless, all-weather roads were far more likely to be found among the nonpoor in 1994, especially those who remained nonpoor during both survey years. Finally, producer prices changed the least for those remaining poor in both survey years and increased the most for those becoming nonpoor. The incidence of serious illness in the household was highest among those remaining poor, and lowest among those becoming nonpoor. Those remaining poor and those becoming poor suffered the highest incidence of poor rains in this period also, while those moving out of poverty experienced the best rains in the five years between the two rounds of the survey.

Table 23 summarizes the extent to which the regression model used for the growth decomposition helps to explain the changes observed for each group. The top of the table gives the mean values, followed by the actual and predicted growth in consumption. The highest growth rate is predicted for those becoming nonpoor and those remaining nonpoor. Growth for the latter group is underestimated considerably, however. Growth of those becoming poor is estimated to be much lower, but still positive, while the data suggest a decline in real consumption. Growth for those remaining poor and remaining nonpoor is, on average, well estimated; the data show the differing fortunes of the poor in 1989. Predicted (and actual) growth of those remaining poor is only about half of the

Table 22. Household Characteristics by Poverty Transition Group

Item		Remained poor	Nonpoor in 1989, became poor in 1994	Nonpoor in 1994, poor in 1989	Remained nonpoor	Overall mean
Outcomes[a]	Real food consumption per adult in 1989 (1994 prices)	19.68	70.77	22.11	75.93	41.05
	Real food consumption per adult in 1994	21.99	26.39	104.81	111.16	64.62
	Real total gross income per adult per month in 1989	13.80	31.13	21.39	42.99	25.25
	Real total gross income per adult per month in 1994	25.55	26.42	39.87	56.70	36.29
Livestock[a]	Real value livestock per adult in 1989	155.32	550.92	344.72	828.89	418.60
	Real value livestock per adult in 1994	265.13	418.39	462.60	736.04	445.26
	Number of livestock units owned per adult in 1989	0.16	0.54	0.33	0.79	0.41
	Number of livestock units owned per adult in 1994	0.38	0.56	0.64	0.89	0.59
Land	Land per adult in 1989	0.34	0.55	0.42	0.66	0.46
	Land per adult in 1994	0.39	0.51	0.55	0.63	0.50
Agricultural potential	Quality of soil (scaled relative to village mean)[b]	1.11	0.93	0.93	0.96	1.00
	Agricultural potential per village (relative to overall mean)[c]	1.01	0.94	1.02	1.00	1.00
	Augmented land per adult (land times quality and potential)	0.29	0.37	0.47	0.53	0.41
Export crops	Chat grown now?	0.07	0.08	0.16	0.26	0.14
	Coffee grown now?	0.35	0.15	0.02	0.05	0.17
Fertilizer	Fertilizer used in 1994	0.57	0.53	0.48	0.60	0.55
	Using more modern inputs than 5 years ago in 1994?	0.11	0.19	0.27	0.29	0.20

Income source[a]	Real crop and land income per adult per month in 1989	7.15	16.55	8.72	20.97	12.14
	Real crop and land income per adult per month in 1994	11.06	10.79	17.99	22.96	15.44
	Real livestock product income per month per adult in 1989	0.32	1.83	1.28	3.61	1.54
	Real livestock product income per month per adult in 1994	0.80	2.07	2.63	5.39	2.49
	Real livestock sale income per adult per month in 1989	1.90	4.55	5.34	8.32	4.66
	Real livestock sale income per adult per month in 1994	6.03	6.20	10.12	16.35	9.40
	Real wage labor income 1989 per adult per month	0.42	1.67	1.39	2.94	1.43
	Rreal wage labor income 1994 per adult per month	1.01	0.44	1.36	1.19	1.04
	Real business income 1989 per adult per month	2.15	4.56	2.38	4.21	3.06
	Real business income 1994 per adult per month	5.61	6.83	6.89	8.78	6.84
	Real private transfers per adult per month in 1989	0.71	0.72	0.92	1.21	0.88
	Real private transfers per adult per month in 1994	1.02	0.10	0.39	1.33	0.78
	Real FFW plus aid income per month per adult 1989	0.07	0.28	0.06	0.09	0.10
	Real FFW plus aid income per month per adult 1994	0.02	0.00	0.50	0.71	0.29
Demographics	Male adults in 1989 (above 15 years)	1.34	1.25	1.41	1.32	1.34
	Male adults in 1994 (above 15 years)	1.99	1.78	1.81	1.68	1.84
	Female adults in 1989 (above 15 years)	1.60	1.39	1.62	1.23	1.49
	Female adults in 1989 (above 15 years)	2.23	2.12	1.63	1.59	1.92
	Adult-equivalent units in household 1989	5.56	4.65	5.42	4.29	5.08
	Adult-equivalent units in household 1994	6.46	5.70	5.35	4.89	5.69

(Table continues on the following page.)

Table 22. (continued)

Item		Remained poor	Nonpoor in 1989, became poor in 1994	Nonpoor in 1994, poor in 1989	Remained nonpoor	Overall mean
	Household size in 1989	6.90	5.71	6.70	5.32	6.29
	Household size in 1994	7.85	6.88	6.46	5.91	6.89
	Male head of household?	0.83	0.83	0.88	0.81	0.84
Education	Head of household completed primary school?	0.02	0.00	0.07	0.02	0.03
	Average years of education of male adults (1994)	0.33	0.43	0.55	0.32	0.40
	Average years of education of female adults (1994)	0.16	0.15	0.20	0.17	0.17
Location	Distance to nearest town by road in km	15.40	13.84	12.46	12.46	13.71
	Any road (tarmac, dirt road) through village?	0.75	0.67	0.62	0.77	0.71
	All-weather road through village?	0.05	0.27	0.36	0.62	0.29
Prices	Percentage change in real producer prices for crops	19.86	28.27	37.70	23.26	26.69
Shocks	Any serious adult illness episodes between 1989 and 1994?	0.71	0.70	0.51	0.55	0.62
	Number of adult illness episodes per adult in family	0.34	0.27	0.21	0.32	0.29
	Short-run rainfall experience (1994 minus 1989)[d]	-0.28	-0.20	-0.11	-0.08	-0.18
	Long-run rainfall experience (1994 minus 1989)[e]	-0.02	-0.02	0.06	0.02	0.01

Note: n = 354. FFW = food for work; this is income derived from public employment programs with payment in the form of food.

a. All values in birr and in 1994 prices.

b. Based on subjective measure, asking farmers to nominate plots as being lem = good, lem-teuf = medium, teuf = poor soil. Land weighted average score, from 0.33 for teuf to 1 for good. Rescaled relative to village mean; that is, difference index relative to mean soil quality.

c. Average village-level potential, based on unit value per kilogram times yield in kilogram per hectare.

d. Difference in percentage deviation from mean in 1994 and 1989. Deviation relative to long-term mean for main season in area. Measure of how good the last main season preceding the 1994 survey was relative to the last mean season preceding the 1989 survey round.

e. Difference in percentage deviation from long-term mean in 1994 and 1989. Rainfall of last five years relative to long-term mean. Measure of how good the last five years were relative to the previous five years.

average growth rate. Predicted growth rates of those becoming nonpoor exceed the average growth by 50 percent. Nevertheless, growth for those changing status is (relatively) poorly estimated, especially for those falling below the poverty line (the smallest group in the sample).

How problematic are these estimates for our analysis? Our main interest is in the effect of reforms and the impact of changes in prices and returns on household welfare. If the poverty transitions were inaccurate because the actual price changes were poorly measured, then this would, of course, be a problem for our analysis. However, the fact that the community fixed effects specification (see table 18) yields virtually identical results confirms that our interpretation is not flawed. In particular, the predicted growth rates of a model with community fixed effects (as in model 3) were also exactly the same, as when using model 6, again underestimating the poverty transitions.

Idiosyncratic shocks and measurement error in the left-side variable are therefore alternative and more likely explanations for the underestimated poverty transitions. As previously discussed, there is little basis to suspect that measurement error is *systematic*; and the issue of idiosyncratic shocks cannot be addressed because of lack of further information for 1989. It would seem reasonable to conclude that the current specification underestimates idiosyncratic shocks considerably, especially in view of evidence that these shocks occur frequently for rural households (on this see Morduch 1999 in general; and Dercon and Krishnan 2000 for information specific to Ethiopia). Yet even without shocks, the growth losses from shocks are high. A simple counterfactual predicted growth rate under unchanged rainfall and no illness suggests that growth was halved by shocks for those remaining poor, and the gap with the average growth rate would have been less than a fifth for them.

The base of table 23 provides evidence on how different groups of people fared differently during this period of high growth. It gives the decomposition for each group, relative to the overall growth in real consumption. Increased returns to infrastructure, price changes, and rainfall are the main variables contributing to the total growth for each group. However, there are some interesting differences between these groups; as to whether the poor benefited from the reforms, it is clear that some groups did so more than others. In particular, the group of poor that

Table 23. Explaining Consumption Changes by Poverty Transition Group

Item	Remains poor	Became poor in 1994	Nonpoor in 1994	Remains nonpoor	Sample
Mean values					
ln(augmented land)	0.06	0.06	0.21	0.33	0.16
Δ ln(land in ha + 0.1)	0.29	0.22	0.49	0.28	0.33
Δ ln(adult equiv.)	0.12	0.18	−0.03	0.12	0.09
ln(years of education per adult)	0.18	0.22	0.25	0.18	0.20
ln(adults serious ill. + 1)	0.23	0.15	0.14	0.20	0.19
Δ (% real prod. prices)	0.20	0.26	0.38	0.23	0.26
Δ ln(rain 5 yrs*seas.)	−0.31	−0.23	−0.07	−0.07	−0.18
ln(distance to town)	0.12	0.05	−0.19	−0.01	0.00
Road infrastructure	0.75	0.67	0.62	0.77	0.71
Predicted and actual change in consumption					
Consumption growth	0.18	-0.78	1.36	0.37	0.37
Predicted change in ln consumption	0.23	0.32	0.52	0.44	0.37
Predicted change in consumption, excl. shocks	0.40	0.45	0.58	0.51	0.48
Percent contribution to mean change in consumption					
Changes in land	0.17	0.13	0.29	0.16	0.19
Changes in labor	0.11	0.17	−0.03	0.12	0.09
Returns to land (technology shift)	0.03	0.03	0.10	0.16	0.08
Returns to education	0.01	0.01	0.01	0.01	0.01
Crop producer price increase	0.32	0.42	0.60	0.37	0.42
Returns to infrastructure and location	0.45	0.45	0.59	0.56	0.51
Illness shocks	−0.12	−0.08	−0.07	−0.10	−0.10
Rainfall shock	−0.35	−0.26	−0.07	−0.08	−0.20
Predicted growth rate as percentage of mean growth	0.62	0.87	1.42	1.20	1.00

Note: n = 354. Decomposition using model 6.

managed to escape poverty could do so because they had more relatively good land of high potential and soil quality, as well as more education; they also benefited from their superior geographical location. The group of poor in 1989 that stayed poor had lower levels of these endowments; also they faced less rainfall since 1989 than the group moving out of poverty in 1989, and they had more illness problems. Those that became poor in 1994 had a relatively poor growth performance because, despite average price increases, they had an inferior geographical location and infrastructure with relatively little good quality land. Relatively poor rains pushed them further into poverty. Finally, the nonpoor throughout did not outperform the average growth rate, which is unusual given the relatively good rainfall in this period. Despite clearly having the best land, the non-poor throughout experienced lower than average producer price increases for the whole sample in this period.

In short, growth appears to have been relatively pro-poor, but not pro-poor throughout; the poor with good land, a good location, and high producer price increases—about a quarter of the sample—benefited more than any other group. On the other hand, a third of the sample—the poorly endowed poor in terms of land and location—experienced the lowest price increases and their benefits from the reforms were limited.

8

Decomposing Poverty Changes

n chapter 6, we presented a decomposition of real income changes for the average household in the sample. In chapter 7, we focused on the experience of groups defined by whether they changed poverty status between 1989 and 1994–95. A decomposition of the factors explaining their income changes was presented in that chapter. In this chapter, we focus on decomposing the change in the overall poverty measures in this sample. We will use the approach developed in chapter 5. In particular, we show that for a well-defined *overall* poverty change, we can identify the contribution of different factors to explain this poverty change by linking a poverty gap measure of poverty to the econometric model of overall real income changes estimated in chapter 6. In this chapter, we will also show some simulations of counterfactuals.[1] For transparency, all results are for the normalized Watts poverty index, that is, the "poverty gap" measure of poverty but using the log of income, rather than the level of income, as the underlying household welfare measure. The actual poverty change of this index was about 29 percent in this period, 1989–95. First, table 24 presents simple microsimulations that show the impact on poverty from the observed total change in each factor (that is, changes in endowments, in returns or shocks, ceteris paribus). As in equations 7 and 13 in chapter 5, counterfactual incomes are derived by adding this factor to real income in 1989 and then looking at the poverty impact in percentages.

Table 24. Microsimulations of the Total Impact of Different Factors on Poverty (Normalized Watts Poverty Index)

Factor	Impact on poverty of observed total change in particular factors (ceteris paribus) in percentages, relative to 1989
Increase in land	−9
Increases in adult labor	−1
Change in returns to land (tech. shift)	0
Changes in returns to education of adults	0
Crop producer price increase	−19
Returns to road infrastructure	−21
Return to location	0
Rainfall shock	12
Illness shocks	5
Change in household size (adult equiv.)	6
Memorandum: total poverty change	−29

Better crop prices and higher returns to roads dominate the results, with even higher percentage effects than when explaining growth. The increase in real producer prices for crops reduced poverty by 19 percent, while the changed returns to road infrastructure reduced poverty by 21 percent. On the other hand, rainfall and illness each appear to have even larger effects on poverty than on growth. The land transfers also have a substantial effect, while the contribution of increased returns to land— probably linked to a shift toward more land-intensive activities—is virtually nil, simply because of the limited amounts or the low potential of land available to the poor.

These simulations consider one particular change as the basis for the counterfactual. As previously noted, one counterfactual is of particular interest: the actual poverty change observed between 1989 and 1994–95 and its contributing factors. Using equation 14 and regression model 6 (table 18), table 25 gives these results: The poverty index used—the poverty gap defined in logs—showed a 29 percent decline in poverty, which is quite similar to the decline in the squared poverty gap reported in table 10, chapter 3. The second column gives the absolute decline in the poverty index by each factor, the third column gives the contribution to the total change in percentages, and the fourth column gives the contribution in percentage points.

Note first that this is not an exact decomposition for the reasons discussed in chapter 5, since the decomposition is only done on a subsample, and the estimating method used for the econometric model only guarantees an exact decomposition for the sample as a whole. However, the residual is very small (less than 1 percent). The main patterns are maintained as before when discussing the decomposition for the sample as a whole (chapter 6), as well as for the contribution to poverty changes

Table 25. Decomposition of the Poverty Gap (Normalized Watts Poverty Index)

Factor	Absolute decline by factor	Contribution to total change	Percent change and contribution in percentage points
Actual poverty change[a]	−0.037	100	−29
Predicted poverty change	−0.038		
Increase in land	−0.013	34	−10
Increases in adult labor	−0.005	13	−4
Change in returns to land (tech. shift)	−0.001	2	0
Changes in returns to education of adults	0.000	1	0
Crop producer price increase	−0.023	62	−18
Returns to road infrastructure	−0.028	76	−22
Return to location	0.002	−4	1
Rainfall shock	0.016	−44	13
Illness shocks	0.006	−16	5
Change in household size (adult equiv.)	0.008	−22	7
Residual	0.000	0	0
Actual poverty gap 1989	0.128		
Actual poverty gap 1994–95	0.089		

a. The actual poverty gap in 1989 was 0.128, declining to 0.089 in 1994.

of specific factors in table 24. The largest contributions come from better crop prices and higher returns to roads. Part of the reason for these high numbers is the large negative impact of shocks; illness and especially rain together contributed to 60 percent of the total poverty gap change. Land increases contributed 34 percent to the observed decline in poverty. Note that this is more than the contribution of land increases to the overall increase in incomes in this sample, which was 19 percent (see table 19). This suggests that the poor benefited more from land increases than the average household in the sample.

The largest part of the poverty decline is driven by one group—those leaving poverty between 1989 and 1994, which constitutes more than 80 percent of the actual poverty decline. Recall from table 23 that this group had relatively good endowments: their crop prices increased the most and they were lucky with ample rains. Those remaining in poverty experienced limited growth; their poverty gap only declined by an insignificant 4 percent. With poor endowments and poorly accessible locations, the increased returns through better prices were limited, and they were virtually wiped out by poor rains and illness.

In table 26, the decomposition of the poverty index is reported by village. The table gives the contribution in terms of percentage points to the total poverty change in each area. With the sample size becoming much smaller, the residuals increase. There are important differences between villages in terms of the determinants of growth. In Dinki, poor rain, poor location, and low land potential resulted in increased poverty, despite large crop producer price increases. Also, the unexplained residual is rather high for this village. In Debre Berhan, despite a relatively low price increase, large land holdings and high returns to its (excellent) location contributed most to the large poverty decline. In Adele Keke, good returns and location contributed most to the poverty decrease. In Korodegaga, the large crop price increase and the increased land holdings after the dissolution of the producer cooperative fueled growth, even though it was tempered by poor rain and its poor location. Gara Godo was the only village to experience a worsening terms of trade for their crops, which contributed to a predicted (and actual) increase in poverty. Insufficient rain exacerbated the problem despite the village's relatively good location. Finally, Domaa's proximity to the town and high price increases con-

Table 26. Poverty Decomposition by Village: Percentage Point Contribution to Total Decline in the Poverty Gap

Factor	Dinki	Debre Berhan	Adele Keke	Koro-degaga	Gara Godo	Domaa	Average
Increase in land	-3	-1	-9	-18	-3	-10	-10
Increases in adult labor	7	-8	5	-2	-10	-3	-4
Change in returns to land	14	-36	14	4	-5	0	0
Changes in returns to education of adults	0	-1	0	0	0	0	0
Price change	-42	-19	-10	-42	21	-20	-18
Returns to road infrastructure/location	-11	-50	-31	-6	-27	-30	-21
Rainfall shock	28	3	-14	24	18	-8	13
Illness shocks	3	1	3	4	5	6	5
Change in adult-equivalent units	-20	22	-15	1	24	1	7
Residual	52	32	-3	-22	-10	23	0
Total change	29	-56	-61	-55	14	-41	-29

tributed to the poverty decline, although the model overestimated this change. In general, the evolution of different household sizes contributed significantly to the observed changes as well.

Table 27 gives the final key table of this report. First, it brings together the factors contributing to actual growth and poverty changes, as reported previously. Then the table reports on two additional counterfactual simulations: one case in which there was no effect from shocks, as if there was full insurance, say through safety nets. The other case is one in which there were no reforms, so that none of the increases in returns nor in prices actually took place. The growth effect is derived simply by excluding these factors from the findings based on the first column of results. Since, as argued before, the poverty decompositions in contributing factors are counterfactual-dependent (that is, they only describe the contributing factors to a particular overall change), they cannot be derived directly from the second column. They are obtained by constructing a spe-

Table 27. Decomposition of Growth per Adult and Poverty Gap: Percentage Point Contribution to Total Growth

Factor	Actual		Counterfactual no risk		Counterfactual no reforms and no peace	
	Growth	Poverty	Growth	Poverty	Growth	Poverty
Increase in land	7	−10	7	−8	1	−2
Increases in adult labor	3	−4	3	−4	3	−4
Change in returns to land (tech.)	3	0	3	−1		
Changes in returns to educated adults	0	0	0	0		
Illness shocks	−4	5			−4	5
Price change	15	−18	15	−16		
Rainfall shock	−8	13			−8	14
Returns to road Infrastructure/location	19	−23	19	−21		
Residual	0	0	0	0	0	3
Change in adult-equiv. units	−5	7	−5	7	−5	7
Percentage growth (sum of above)	32	−29	42	−44	−13	23

cific counterfactual distribution and then applying the decomposition as in equations 14 and 15.[2]

Total per adult growth (defined by the change in the logs of per adult consumption) was 32 percent, while the poverty gap declined by 29 percent. The table gives the contribution in percentage points to this change. Since the percentage change in both per adult growth and poverty is very close in absolute terms (suggesting a scaled Watts poverty elasticity of −0.90), the percentages can be directly compared.

From table 27 it can be concluded that growth in these villages was largely fueled by the reforms and probably helped by peace; better crop prices and better returns to location explain most of the growth. Poverty reduction is determined by similar factors, but poor rains for some groups hindered the decline. Crop price increases, a factor most directly linked to the reforms, contributed more to the decline in poverty than to growth.

The poor benefited somewhat more than proportionately from better returns to roads, even though the poor include a group that is quite remote with poor infrastructure. Poor households in this sample grew in size at more than an average rate, which contributed to lower per adult growth and higher poverty; there is a return through additional labor. Land increases for some of the poor meant that this increase in land holding disproportionately contributed to poverty reduction, but given the current (relatively equal) land distribution within communities and the history of land reform in Ethiopia, this is not easily repeatable nor desirable as a strategy. Since the poor typically have low quality or little land, they could not benefit from the increased returns to land, relative to the average household. Finally, the poor suffered disproportionately from illness shocks and were also unlucky with rain, which limited the decline of poverty further.

The full insurance simulation assumes that all shocks (rainfall and illness) were insured, so that their negative impact would not have taken place. The results suggest large effects on growth and poverty; growth would have been higher by a third, while poverty reduction would have been about 50 percent higher. Insurance, say, in the form of properly functioning safety nets, would clearly add substantially to poverty reduction and growth. The other counterfactual result is to speculate, using the econometric model, what the consequences for growth and poverty reduction would have been if policies had not changed. We discussed in previous chapters (including in chapters 2 and 6) that it is hard to fully disentangle the effects of the economic reform program and the increased security after the end of the war in 1991. This is especially the case for the contribution of the changes in the returns to roads and location to overall real income and poverty changes. As a consequence, the only feasible way to conduct a counterfactual simulation of the outcomes if the economic reform program had not taken place, would be to do so under the assumption that the positive impact of the change in security also did not occur. Recall from our discussion in chapter 2, however, that the impact on prices appears to have been largely from liberalizing measures and not from increased security, so we can have a reasonable degree of confidence that the counterfactual simulation will show mainly the costs on real incomes and poverty of not implementing the economic reform program.

To implement this simulation, we assume that there would have been no changes in the returns to roads and location, and that real producer prices remained unchanged between 1989 and 1994–95 returns. Since incentives did not change, we assume that there is no change in the marginal returns to land because of a change in the technology. What is left are the changes in the levels of assets (land and labor) and shocks. The poor local rainfall in a few villages, illness shocks, and population growth are predicted to have resulted in a 13 percent decline in per adult consumption and a 23 percent increase in poverty. Most of this increase in poverty is for poor who were poor in 1989 and in 1994–95 in our survey data remained poor; those who actually moved out of poverty would have experienced zero poverty growth in this counterfactual scenario. This confirms that even if reforms did not benefit all poor households in the same way, *no* reforms would clearly have made the plight of this persistently poor group even worse.

NOTES

1. Poverty measurement is done in terms of consumption per adult equivalent, while the analysis in the previous section was done in terms of total household consumption. The regressions in chapter 6 were run in terms of total household consumption. Poverty measurement requires a correction for household size, for example, in terms of adult-equivalent units; the decomposition must take this into account. Define aeu_{it} as the number of adult-equivalent units in household i, in year t, and $y_{it} = \ln c_{it} / aeu_{it}$, then we can define

$$(\text{A.5}) \quad P_1 - P_0 = -\frac{1}{n}\sum_{i=1}^{q_{10}} s_i\left(\frac{\ln c_{i1} - \ln c_{i0}}{z}\right) + \frac{1}{n}\sum_{i=1}^{q_{10}} s_i\left(\frac{\ln aeu_{i1} - \ln aeu_{i0}}{z}\right)$$

so that a decomposition of changes of poverty simply requires an additional term that corrects for changes in household adult-equivalent units.

2. The decomposition of growth is repeated, but this time in terms of per adult real consumption. This simply implies an additional term defined by (minus) the change in the log of the number of adult-equivalent units in both years.

9

Conclusions

I n this text, the poverty and growth experience of six villages in rural Ethiopia were studied in the period 1989 to 1994–95. In 1989, these six villages had suffered from the famine years of the mid-1980s, and were barely starting to recover. At the same time, the economy around them was in disarray. The collapse of the economy at the end of the war in 1990–91 contributed to the fact that the Ethiopian economy did not grow much between 1989 and 1994–95 in terms of GDP per capita. The national accounts still showed some growth, 14 percent in consumption, largely due to the collapse in government expenditure and investment. The study villages experienced much higher growth rates, well above the national trend, although this is partially explained by the relatively low levels of consumption observed at the end of the 1980s. The available evidence on the main liquid asset, livestock, suggests that these villages had barely returned to the prefamine levels in 1989, so living standards in 1994–95 were unlikely to be much higher than in the period before the famine of 1984–85.

The period studied in this text, 1989 to 1994–95, was a period of considerable change in economic policies relevant for the rural sector. Measures included the liberalization of food markets, a decline in rural taxation, a large devaluation in 1992, and less repression of the private sector in the economy. The effects of these economic policy changes are traced from the macrolevel to the local level. Food market reform, changes in different forms of taxation, and (to a lesser extent) the devaluation contributed to improved producer crop prices in all but one village; on average, the prices increased by 26 percent. The effects of the devaluation on exportables are somewhat convoluted owing to the presence of large-scale smuggling of chat, and to some extent coffee, which implies that the actual prices obtained by farmers may not have improved very much. Formal land reform had ended by 1988, but in one village some farmers gained substantial amounts of land because of the dissolution of the producer cooperative in 1991. Fertilizer reform was not found to have much impact on farmers' incomes.

The war of the mid-1980s to early 1990s had only a limited direct effect on the villages and the surrounding areas. The externalities from increased security across large parts of the country after 1992 cannot easily be calculated, but they probably contributed to real incomes via increased returns to roads and location. Rains were (somewhat surprisingly) found to be little better in the period 1990–94 than in the preceding five years; a localized drought in 1993–94 in parts of central and southern Ethiopia affected some of the villages studied.

Food consumption grew strongly in all but one village, on average, by more than 8 percent per year. Poverty declined in four villages and increased in the two others. Poverty fell more for some of the poorest households; the headcount index fell by 16 percent, but the squared poverty gap fell by 31 percent. Poverty remains high, nevertheless; the headcount index in 1994–95 was still more than 50 percent.

Inequality increased, but the panel data show that to some extent this assessment may be misleading. The poorest households (the lowest decile) in 1989 had, on average, the highest growth rates; growth rates appear to have been monotonically declining by decile. However, mean consumption per adult for the lowest decile in 1994 compared to that for the lowest decile in 1989 had increased by less than the mean growth rate (by a fifth less). This was, in general, the case for the lowest half of the distribution. Behind these seemingly puzzling results is a lot of movement across the consumption distribution, with a substantial number of households moving out of poverty, and a smaller group falling below the poverty line.

Can growth be linked to the reforms? A reduced-form household fixed effects "profit" function was estimated, linking real income to fixed endowments of land and labor, as well as prices, returns to location, and shocks. The model allows for changes in the returns to assets between 1989 and 1994. The evidence presented suggests that increased producer crop prices are directly linked to the reforms and play a large part in explaining growth. Furthermore, there appears to be a growth effect from a shift back to agriculture, especially on good quality land of high potential, consistent with the change toward more favorable policies toward the agricultural sector, with better prices and lower taxation. Higher returns to roads and good location contribute to growth and are consistent with the increased encouragement of market-oriented activities (even though, in this case, these higher returns to roads and location are also likely to be a reflection of a peace-dividend).

Has this growth been pro-poor? On average, yes. But, more accurately, it has been pro-poor for some, not for others. The poor are heterogeneous and at least two groups can be distinguished in 1989. A first group—about a third of the sample, or half the poor—had been blessed with good rains and good land, they faced high crop producer price increases, and they had good access to roads and towns. They outperformed the rest of the sample in terms of growth, and they contributed more than 80 percent to the overall estimated reduction in the poverty gap. The other group—the other half of the poor in 1989—stayed poor in both sample years and had much lower growth, about a third below average. They did not manage to grow as much because of their land endowment, which was either small or of poor potential, and they typically lived in remote areas with poor road connections. For this second group, most of the benefit from the reforms was wiped out by poor rains and illness shocks. This group is not identical to the poorest households in 1989, even though they were more likely to come from the lowest deciles.[1]

Have the reforms been pro-poor? Yes, but again, they have been pro-poor for some of the poor. The decomposition of the (normalized Watts) poverty gap index showed that crop price increases and higher returns to infrastructure actually contributed more to the percentage decline in the poverty gap than to growth. But this mainly benefited some—those with better endowments in terms of land and location. Some of the households with the poorest endowments, such as poor location, did not obtain much better crop output prices from the reforms.

It is clear that the same factors seem to be driving growth and poverty. But this also constrains any poverty reduction through growth. By 1994, the poor included households with poor endowments in terms of land, distance from towns, or road infrastructure. While better rains or favorable movements in relative prices still provide opportunities for some of these households to move out of poverty, additional opportunities may be necessary. These poor households are unlikely to respond strongly to increased incentives or to experience these increased incentives in the form of higher output prices or returns. This is reflected in the poverty-growth elasticity; it is well below one for all the poverty measures discussed. High growth for this poorly endowed group does not yield more than a proportionate percentage decline in poverty.

The counterfactuals discussed also highlight the role played by risk; for example, poor rains in the years preceding the 1994 survey are an important factor limiting growth for some of the poor. The growth benefits from better insurance systems and safety nets and from better savings and credit markets could be high (see Dercon forthcoming).

Despite the fact that reforms do not deliver similar benefits to all the poor, the results indicate the high costs linked to withholding reforms. If there had been no reforms (and peace), returns to assets and real relative prices would have remained as they were in 1989. In that case, per adult consumption would have declined further and poverty would have increased by a fifth. Some of the poorest would have been the worst affected, because they also faced the largest negative shocks during this period. These poorest households also typically remained poor in 1994–95 in the actual data. Even though they may not have benefited as much as others from the reforms, they would have suffered more had the reforms not taken place.

NOTE

1. Two-thirds of the poorest two deciles stayed poor in 1994, while half of the fifth decile stayed poor.

References

Ayalew, D., S. Dercon, and P. Krishnan. 1999. "Demobilisation, Land and House-hold Livelihoods: Lessons from Ethiopia." Research in Progress RIP24, World Institute for Development Economics Research, United Nations University, Helsinki, December.

Azam, J. P. 1993. "La Levée des Côntroles des Marchés de Grains en Ethiopie (Mars 1990)." Revue d'Economie du Développement 94 (3) : 79–104.

———. 1994. "The Uncertain Distributional Impact of Structural Adjustment in Sub-Saharan Africa." In R. Van der Hoeven and F. Van der Kraaij, eds., Structural Adjustment and Beyond: Long-term Development in Sub-Saharan Africa. Oxford: James Currey Publishers.

———. 1996. "The Diversity of Adjustment in Agriculture." In S. Ellis, ed., Africa Now. Oxford: James Currey Publishers.

Azam, J. P., D. Bevan, P. Collier, S. Dercon, J. W. Gunning, and S. Pradhan. 1994. "Some Economic Consequences of the Transition from Civil War to Peace." Policy Research Working Paper 1392. World Bank, Policy Research Department, Washington, D.C.

Blinder, A. 1973. "Wage Discrimination: Reduced Form and Structural Estimates." Journal of Human Resources 8 : 436–55.

Bourguignon, F., J. de Melo, and C. Morrisson. 1991. "Poverty and Inequality Distribution during Adjustment: Issues and Evidence from the OECD Project." World Development 19 : 1485–1508.

Bourguignon, F., M. Fournier, and M. Grugnand. 2001. "Fast Development with a Stable Income Distribution: Taiwan, 1979–1994." Review of Income and Wealth 47: 139–63.

Braverman, A., and J. S. Hammer. 1986. "Multimarket Analysis of Agricultural Pricing Policies." In I. Singh, L. Squire, and J. Strauss, eds., Agricultural Household Models, Extensions, Applications and Policy. Baltimore: Johns Hopkins University Press.

Cornia, G. A., R. Jolly, and F. Stewart, eds. 1987. Adjustment with a Human Face. Oxford: Oxford University Press.

Datt, G., and M. Ravallion. 1992. "Growth and Redistribution Components of Changes in Poverty Measures: A Decomposition with Applications to Brazil and India in the 1980s." *Journal of Development Economics* 38 : 275–95.

De Janvry, A., and E. Sadoulet. 1995. *Quantitative Development Policy Analysis.* Baltimore: Johns Hopkins University Press.

De Janvry, A., E. Sadoulet, and M. Fafchamps. 1991. "Peasant Household Behaviour with Missing Markets." *Economic Journal* 101 : 1400–17.

Deaton, A. 1997. *The Analysis of Household Surveys: a Microeconometric Approach to Development Policy.* Baltimore: Johns Hopkins University Press.

Demery, L., and L. Squire. 1996. "Macroeconomic Adjustment and the Poverty in Africa: An Emerging Picture." *World Bank Research Observer* 11 (1) : 39–59.

Dercon, S. 1994. "The Consequences of Liberalisation and Peace for Food Markets in Ethiopia." In *Some Economic Consequences of the Transition from Civil War to Peace.* Policy Research Working Paper 1392. The World Bank Policy Research Department, Public Economics Division, Washington, D.C.

———.1995. "On Market Integration and Liberalisation : Method and Application to Ethiopia." *Journal of Development Studies* 32 (1) : 112–43.

———. 2001. *Economic Reform, Growth, and the Poor: Evidence from Rural Ethiopia.* Working Paper Series 2001.7. Centre for the Study of African Economics, Oxford University, United Kingdom.

———. Forthcoming. "Income Risk, Coping Strategies and Safety Nets." World Bank, *World Bank Research Observer.*

Dercon S., and Daniel Ayalew. 1998. "Where Have All the Soldiers Gone: Demobilization and Reintegration in Ethiopia." *World Development* 26 (9) : 1661–76.

Dercon, S., and Lulseged Ayalew. 1995. "Smuggling and Supply Response: Coffee in Ethiopia." *World Development* 23 (10) : 1795–1813.

Dercon, S., and P. Krishnan. 1996. "Income Portfolios in Rural Ethiopia and Tanzania: Choices and Constraints." Journal of Development Studies 32 (6) : 850–75.

———. 1998. "Changes in Poverty in Rural Ethiopia 1989–1995: Measurement, Robustness Tests and Decomposition." Working Paper Series 98.7. Centre for the Study of African Economies, Oxford University, United Kingdom.

———. 2000. "Vulnerability, Seasonality and Poverty in Ethiopia." *Journal of Development Studies* 36 (6): 25–53.

Dessalegn, Rahmato. 1991. *Famine and Survival Strategies: A Case Study from Northeast Ethiopia.* Uppsala, Sweden: Nordiska Afrikainstitutet.

Dollar, D., and A. Kraay. 2000. "Growth Is Good for the Poor." Washington, D.C.: World Bank. Processed.

Foster, J., J. Greer, and E. Thorbecke. 1984. "A Class of Decomposable Poverty Measures." *Econometrica* 52 (1): 761–66.

Glewwe, P., and G. Hall. 1994. "Are Some Groups More Vulnerable to Macroeconomic Shock than Others? Hypothesis Tests Based on Panel Data from Peru." *Journal of Development Economics* 56 (1) : 181–206.

Grootaert, C. 1995. "Structural Change and Poverty in Africa: A Decomposition Analysis for Côte d'Ivoire." *Journal of Development Economics* 47 : 375–401.

Grootaert, C., and R. Kanbur. 1995. "The Lucky Few Amidst Economic Decline: Distributional Change in Côte D'Ivoire as Seen through Panel Data Sets, 1985–88." *Journal of Development Studies* 31 (4) : 603–19.

IMF (International Monetary Fund). 2000. *International Financial Statistics.* Washington, D.C.: IMF.

Kakwani, N. 1993a. "Poverty and Economic Growth with Application to Côte d'Ivoire." *Review of Income and Wealth* 39 (2) : 121–39.

———. 1993b. "Statistical Inference in the Measurement of Poverty." *Review of Economics and Statistics* LXXV : 632–39.

Kanbur, S. M. R. 1987. "Structural Adjustment, Macroeconomic Adjustment and Poverty: a Methodology for Analysis." *World Development* 15 (12) : 1515–26.

Lipton, M., and M. Ravallion. 1995. "Poverty and Policy." In J. Behrman and T. N. Srinivasan, eds., *Handbook of Development Economics.* Amsterdam: Elsevier Science B.V.

Morduch, J. 1999. "Informal Insurance between the State and the Market." *World Bank Research Observer* 14 (2): 187–207.

Mulat, Demeke, Ali Said, and T. S. Jayne. 1997. "Promoting Fertilizer Use in Ethiopia." Grain Market Research Project, Working Paper 5. Ministry of Economic Development and Cooperation, Ethiopia.

———. 1998. "Agricultural Market Performance and Determinants of Fertilizer Use in Ethiopia." Grain Market Research Project, Working Paper 10. Ministry of Economic Development and Cooperation, Ethiopia.

Oaxaca, R. 1973. "Male-Female Wage Differentials in Urban Labor Markets." *International Economic Review* 9 : 693–709.

Ravallion, M. 1994. *Poverty Comparisons.* Chur, Switzerland: Harwood Academic Publishers.

Ravallion, M., and B. Bidani. 1994. "How Robust Is a Poverty Profile?" *The World Bank Economic Review* 8 (1) : 75–102.

Ravallion, M., and G. Datt. 2000. "When Is Growth Pro-poor? Evidence from the Diverse Experiences of India's States." Development Research Group Working Paper Series 2263. World Bank, Washington, D.C.

Sahn, D., ed. 1994. *Adjusting to Policy Failure in African Economies.* Ithaca, New York: Cornell University Press.

————.1996. *Economic Reform and the Poor in Africa*. Oxford: Clarendon Press.

Singh, I., L. Squire, and J. Strauss. 1986. *Agricultural Household Models, Extensions, Applications and Policy*. Baltimore: Johns Hopkins University Press.

Srinivasan, T. N. 2000. "Growth and Poverty Alleviation: Lessons from Development Experience." Asian Development Bank, Manila, Philippines. Processed.

Webb, P., J. von Braun, and Y. Yohannes. 1992. "Famine in Ethiopia: Policy Implication of Coping Failure at National and Household Levels." *Research Report no. 92*. International Food Policy Research Institute, Washington, D.C.